D1508936

Praise for A Down to Earth God

"Garry Genser's devotionals capture vivid spiritual insights from common daily experiences. They will help you to see the leading hand of God in your life and inspire you to a greater commitment to His will."

-Samuele Bacchiocchi, Ph. D.,
Retired Professor of Theology and Church History, Andrews University

"I have used Garry Genser's inspirational stories for our family worships. Get ready for refreshing insights and for your love and appreciation of God to grow."

-Steve Case
President of Piece of the Pie Ministries, Former Youth Ministry Professor & Youth Resource Center Director at Andrews University

"...An unpretentious, humorous writing style that is as easy to read as it is uplifting!"

-Jim Pedersen
President of the Northern California Conference of Seventh-day Adventists

A Down to Earth God

DEVOTIONALS FOR THE NATURE LOVER

Garry Genser

New Life Publishing House

Published by New Life Publishing House, P.O. Box 67 Hydesville, California 95547

SAN: >>>>>>>>>   8 5 0 – 8 8 4 4   <<<<<<<<<<<

All scriptures are from the King James Version unless marked with "My Translation". Some spelling has been modified from the Old English by the author.

Library of Congress-in-Publication Data

Cataloging Control Number: 2006926524

ISBN-13: 978-0-9785573-0-0

Printed in the United States of America

Contents

Dedication

No man is an island and no author writes a book alone. In my case I had my loving wife, Suzanne, and two marvelous secretaries, Marie Aldinger and Dolores Gardener, without whose editing this book would have been left high and dry and to whom I am eternally grateful.

Introduction

God speaks to us, not only in the thunderous voice of the prophets or in the majestic and deep scriptures of our Bibles but also in a still small, down to earth voice. Elijah taught us that God speaks to us in the quiet times between the storms of our lives.

In the non-fiction stories of this book I have shared how God has spoken to me in the joys and sorrows of life on a small ranch in Humboldt county along the Northern California coast. I hope that you will be moved to listen to God more clearly as He speaks to you in the daily circumstances of your life and that the Holy Scriptures take on a richer, more relevant meaning because of your new adventures in listening to the still small voice of a down to earth God.

....And, behold, the LORD passed by, and a great and strong wind rent the mountains, and brake in pieces the rocks before the LORD; but the LORD was not in the wind: and after the wind an earthquake; but the LORD was not in the earthquake: And after the earthquake a fire; but the LORD was not in the fire: and after the fire a still small voice. -1 Kings 19:11-12.

The Three Goats from Hell

My dream of owning land has finally come true. Sure, it's along a busy highway, under the approach to the runway of the Fortuna airport, next to the railroad tracks, and on the side of a steep hill but it's still land— God's, the bank's, and mine. I sometimes walk over to the little orchard planted too close to the overshadowing redwoods and sugar pines and pick a diminutive apple or pear and eat it with the relish that only landowners know. Munching between the holes and bites already made by other critters, I smile deep inside, acknowledging that God and I made that pear grow. Isn't it good?

But with this expansive, Lord-of-the-domain feeling also comes the awareness of having to care for the place. Oh, I wish I had cut those huge, thistly-looking purple flowers before they exploded into the seedy beginnings of next year's weeds. And what about keeping the grass and brush down? Horses have no income-producing value but would be so much fun. Cows would work very well with the sketchy fencing I have but eating them wouldn't be very good for my cholesterol. Goats would eat the brush, poison oak, and grass just fine but my fencing isn't adequate. Oh, what to do, what to do. I really don't have much time to spend on this, with pastoring a new church and so many people to visit.

So you can see why I would be delighted to look out one morning to see three little white goats munching contentedly on my thistles and weeds down in my lower field. I later went down to visit them and we negotiated a fifteen-foot relationship consisting of my talking soothing nonsense and their staring at me blankly and chewing. It was so *country*! I immediately began praising God for taking care of even this smallest of needs.

The next day the furry threesome felt more comfortable and ventured even closer. After a couple of days I looked out my bedroom window and the three cute goats were kneeling in the shade of the nearby maple tree looking as comfortable as could be. What have I done to be so loved by God and so blessed without even asking?

The next day I noted with satisfaction that the goats came even closer. They were eating the patch of weeds watered by the leech lines in front of my house, where the rains will eventually reveal a lawn. The goats looked extremely well fed. I walked gently around them toward my tiny orchard to grab a pear for Suzanne and an apple for myself. The solitary red delicious apple I had been leaving to grow a little bigger near the top of an otherwise bare dwarf tree was missing! It screamed of violence like a bank vault door hanging crookedly off its hinges. My apple was missing!

And my pears—the whole tree full—were all gone,

except for a few half-eaten ones! The upper branches were broken and hanging down at sickly angles. And those blasted goats, looking bloated, smiled nearby and practically belched with satisfaction. Later that evening my neighbor stopped by and said the highway patrol had found those same three goats stopping traffic on Highway 36 after having almost caused who-knows-how-many accidents.

Why do we interpret anything that appears to be positive as a blessing from God when the same blessing may soon turn out to be a curse? It occurs to me that instead of relying on the better hope the scriptures promise, we let our spirituality hang in the balance of day-to-day events. If this or that happens in my favor God is blessing me. It suddenly seems more mature to keep in mind *...for he maketh his sun to rise on the evil and on the good, and sendeth rain on the just and on the unjust* (Matthew 5:45).

God promises that *all* things work toward our good, if we love Him. We need not ride the crest of positive events as if they are evidence of God's love in our lives any more than we should allow the negative events, the death and disease which surround us, to become indicators of God's disfavor. Let the goats in our life be neither the goats from God nor the goats from hell. Let them simply be goats, and let God be God, yearning to lead us home, and able to use ANY circumstances in our life to our long-term advantage. Isn't that the real miracle?

Laughing Spiders

No one told me about all the spiders. They must love the country life too, judging by the way they prosper! Having a barn-red house makes their webs really stand out. I was thankful when Frank, the former owner of our new house, decided to leave his pressure washer with the house. Boy, how those pesky arachnids scattered as I reclaimed lost territory and brought the light of day once more to the trim and gutters which were actually white after all.

Running low on oil, I faithfully and enthusiastically filled it up. I filled it up until its cup "runneth over." I filled it up with so much oil that it couldn't take the pressure and starting it back up it made the worst clanking sounds, belching huge clouds of bluish-gray smoke everywhere. With a rattling and horribly abrupt clatter, it stopped. It stopped and wouldn't start, not even allowing me to pull the rope.

The former owner, who likes to come over a couple times a week, suggested I might have overfilled it with oil, so we poured some out. He got it to sometimes let the rope be pulled, but I knew I had done it in and it would now need to have the engine rebuilt. I started researching places that rebuilt small gas engines. It was so discouraging to have a broken engine standing in my driveway with all the spiders looking on, probably laughing, and pointing with their jagged legs at the naive city slicker!

Every time I passed the pressure washer I reviewed my folly, moved it farther out of the way, disconnected the water supply or gave the rope a pull. After several days of finally just letting it alone, I gave the rope a pull and the machine coughed a little puffy, asthmatic cough. I pulled the rope again and it coughed again, but this time a tiny little blue cloud came out, evidence that a spark had occurred. A little oil dripped out of the muffler. A couple more pulls and a bluish, oily cloud grew like a fog in a science fiction movie as the engine began to burn off the congested, overfilled oil. Five minutes later, I was once again the terror of the spider community.

Sometimes we want to accomplish a lot of things in a hurry. In our zeal we put too much oil in our engines and they get clogged and can't breathe. Too much back pressure in our crankcases. I often need to remember: "God makes all things beautiful in his time." He does want us to have urgency about doing His will, but He doesn't want us to clog up our engines with too much pressure either. And if we do clog things up isn't it wonderful to have a Lord who understands our follies and offers us peace? All we have to do is give it a rest and leave things to Him.

God teaches us about the importance of resting in the fourth of the Ten Commandments. Did you know that "Sabbath" means "rest?" Isn't it interesting that the commandment that has to do with rest is the only commandment that begins with the word "remember?" *Remember the Sabbath day by keeping it holy. Six days you shall labor and do all your work, but the seventh day is a Sabbath to the LORD your God. On it you shall not do any work, neither you, nor your son or daughter, nor your manservant or maidservant, nor your animals, nor the alien within your gates. For in six days the LORD made the heavens and the earth, the sea, and all that is in them, but he rested on the seventh day. Therefore the LORD blessed the Sabbath day and made it holy* (Ex 20:8-11).

Living Springs

Somewhere in a muddy patch of blackberry bushes, poison oak and weeds there was supposed to be a spring. The only real evidence of the spring was that I needed to put a board down to not get my feet muddy when I walked the path down to the lower field of my property. I had a friend come to visit me and since he had built roads and knew all about machinery, I thought he would be able to tell me the perfect piece of equipment to use to clear my land and make my little heaven on earth blossom. He told me that my property was so steep I probably needed something with tracks rather than with wheels and my vision began to evaporate.

My new friend, Don said, "You have to clear out that kind of thing by hand. Maybe you could use a little poison, maybe a little burning, but basically you have to clear it by hand." By hand! By *my* hand! Clear those thorny, scratchy, and totally obnoxious-looking branches, one by one, with my hands! My allergies are so bad I break out into a rash just thinking about it. I began to think of the virtues of untouched blackberry bushes. Poison oak turns a pretty red in the fall and the untouched white berries began to seem attractive as well.

Enter the picture, Jeff—young, wide shouldered, unafraid of challenges and of poison oak. I was unsure whether his eagerness was evidence of his inexperience or of his ability and bravery, until after a couple of hours of work, when a hole appeared in the dense, matted hillside. My vision of a clean spring began to re-emerge—not just a spring, but also a grotto, a shrine to all things hopeful and beautiful, a landmark of things able to be built and accomplished. We stood together peering into the little clearing and imagined a wonderful place, sheltered from the wind, with planted ferns and benches next to this beautiful spring. He stuck a stick into the muddy ground, into the future crystalline spring, like an unwaving flag on the surface of the moon.

Oh, youth, source of wonder and of hope! God's work will be finished by such as these. Together let us encourage, guide and put our trust and hope in our youth. I hope they know how treasured they are. From the muddy banks of our present sinful world, our youth will lead the world to the shores of the river of life. *And it shall come to pass afterward, [that] I will pour out my spirit upon all flesh; and your sons and your daughters shall prophesy, your old men shall dream dreams, your young men shall see visions* (Joel 2:28). *The wolf also shall dwell with the lamb, and the leopard shall lie down with the kid; and the calf and the young lion and the fatling together; and a little child shall lead them* (Isaiah 11:6).

The Pastures of our Lives

I never thought I would be able to own a horse. She's not exactly a racehorse. The scar across her face, evidence she had lost an argument with a barbed-wire fence some time in her past, probably made her more affordable. Her previous owners called her Tammy. My wife suggested Tammy Fae, but I confess I just couldn't bear hearing myself calling out, "Tammy Fae! Tammy Fae!" from my porch every morning. Therefore I adapted her name to what I did feel comfortable yelling from my front porch: "Hey Girl!" Or maybe it should be "Hay Girl!" because she does love to eat.

Anyway, she's a lovely unregistered sorrel quarter horse with a blonde mane and an independent spirit. Blonde, independent, and spirited; hmm mm, I'd better let that one go or my wife, Suzanne, will think I'm writing about her.

I'm trying to get her to be friends with my wife with the ultimate goal in mind of being able to go riding together. Suzanne and Hey Girl both being independent and spirited, were most likely each waiting for the other to say "Hi" first. Recently I rode Hey Girl up to our back porch as Suzanne was coming in from work. Previous experience told me that would be easier than getting Suzanne to go to Hey Girl. I could only get Hey Girl to approach within a few feet of the strange surroundings because she kept shying away. She was afraid of the non-horse-friendly brick steps and iron railing.

Suzanne, sensing her fear, added it to her own and could just barely bring herself to stiffly pet Hey Girl on the forehead, following my instructions carefully and reluctantly. It wasn't exactly the kind of moment that would bring tears to your eyes or make you think of scenes from "My Friend, Flicka" or "Black Beauty".

Horses and people aren't at their best in strange surroundings where unknown dangers may lurk. This makes it easier to understand why a growing church reaches outward into the community rather than sitting back waiting for people to come to it. Let those who have the peace and joy found only in the Spirit of the Lord venture out into the currents of life and attract the wounded, the hurt and the sick, to the health radiating from Christ within.

My horse follows me now and likes to be where I am because it associates my presence with food, fellowship, and security. At first though, I had to go out into the pasture where she felt comfortable. ...*This is what the psalmist meant when he wrote: 'I will praise you among the Gentiles, I will sing praises to your name'* (Romans 15:9).

We, Like Cows

We, like sheep, have gone astray. You know the expression. You know how often the Bible uses sheep to describe our human nature with its weakness and foibles, compounded and multiplied when several human beings are put together. Let's face it—we act funny.

Well, I'm not in a position to comment on sheep, because I haven't observed them much, except to note that some owners, like the horse trainer/sheep-raising lady I met recently in Bayside, put jackets on them. It's odd to see sheep, with a thick coat of wool, destined to be made into warm sweaters or jackets, wearing polyester parkas.

I don't know much about sheep, other than these polyester-clad critters, but I have had the privilege of observing cows lately. My neighbor with the pumpkin patch and corn maize has turned his spent fields over to a herd of cattle, and now Suzanne and I watch the spectacle of cow society from our living room couch.

The cows are spread out all over the 18 acre field. Sometimes one cow gets spooked and runs a few feet.

Others nearby, watching the spooked cow, can't seem to stop themselves from running a few feet in sympathy. Then the entire herd of cows, in a giant chain reaction, runs in the same direction. They gather together in the eastern triangle of fencing where they are so crowded and the grass so trampled that there couldn't possibly be enough for any one cow to eat. After a while, some brave soul ventures out, and the entire herd follows single file. They each eventually forget what they were doing and wander off distracted by greener grass.

In church life, I've seen the same thing again and again. We, like cows, have gone astray. Sometimes it's not even the most important or influential leader-types that lead people off on some soon forgotten parade till they are self-corralled in some tight corner with little nourishment. I think we all have that capacity to spook others and lead them off in some foolish, pointless meandering.

Knowing that we have this effect on each other places a responsibility on us to be aware of our behavior. We might afford wasting time in a crowded, muddy corner of the field, but what about our neighbor who might be sickly and may need to feed undisturbed in order to recover from some illness more effectively?

And it is wise, of course, to keep our eyes on God and to go where He wants us to go, rather than to waste our time chasing confused and easily spooked cattle. *But when he saw the multitudes, he was moved with compassion on them, because they fainted, and were scattered abroad, as sheep having no shepherd* (Matthew 9:36).

Little Cracks Let in Big Storms

The electricity was out to the north and to the south of us. Our windows shook with the force of the wind funneled through the Van Duzen River valley. A sliding glass door had been mistakenly left open three quarters of an inch. Through that crack the wind was able to create a pressure vacuum causing the large windowpanes in the living room to bend inward and then back outward as the wind blew and sucked.

I sat there watching the increasingly drastic stress on the windows, at times expecting the pane to completely give way. The previous owner, in order to save some money, had replaced some broken double pane windows with single panes of glass held in place with double-sided tape. Knowing about the flimsy method of attaching the glass aroused my imagination as to what may happen if the winds blew any harder. Finally, I noticed the slightly open door and closed it. The windstorm continued to howl outside but we were safe and the house became quiet and calm.

Leaving little things undone, like closing the door all

the way, makes our peace and security so much more vulnerable to the winds of strife. Things like that seem so small and petty and we wonder why we should have to bother with such trivial details. But, when we find ourselves watching the glass walls of our lives bulge inward and flex outward, like they are going to burst, it is a relief when we notice the cause and can fix the problem so easily.

How much time do we waste in worry and want because of small neglects, little matters of diet and exercise, details in tithes and offerings, consistency in devotionals and prayer? How much more rested and more successful in the important things in our lives would we be if we didn't have to stress over the commotion caused by the neglect of small details? *Woe unto you, scribes and Pharisees, hypocrites! For ye pay tithe of mint and anise and cumin, and have omitted the weightier [matters] of the law, judgment, mercy, and faith: these ought ye to have done, and not to leave the other undone* (Matthew 23:23). *For who hath despised the day of small things?* (Zechariah 4:10).

Big Guy

While walking in the Eureka mall about ten years ago, I passed by a shiny storefront window and saw a fellow with a rather unbalanced-looking profile. He was thin all over except for his stomach, which bulged out enough to look a little funny, or so it seemed, until I realized that it was MY reflection.

It shocked me. In that upset state, my denial mechanisms were so weakened that some facts on health and nutrition actually got through to me... like the unreasonableness of skipping breakfast, thinking it would make me lose weight, and then rewarding myself with a bag of potato chips for my victory over my appetite. I began to focus on other health principles that I had been neglecting.

Ten years later and reasonably healthy, I stood in line at an Office Depot and a kid, trying to be friendly and casual said, "Whatcha need today, Big Guy?" *Big Guy?* I mumbled some response and then felt uneasy all that day. That evening, munching on more potato chips than I've allowed myself in years, I still mulled over the thought of being referred to as "Big Guy." Despite all my efforts, munch, I still come across that way? Munch, munch....

Worrying about being fat makes you want to eat more. Getting excited about health or active living tends to keep you thinner. Likewise, focusing on sin, whether avoiding it or pursuing it, sometimes just leads to more of it. Focusing on God, whether by wrestling with Him like Jacob, or following His star like a wise man, leads to greater Godliness. *Seek Ye first the kingdom of God and His Righteousness and all these things shall be added unto you* (Matthew 6:33).

Before the Fall

I had never seen anything like it, well, maybe once before, but that was a two-legged creature, not a horse. Hey Girl never had the rich feed I started giving her before—all kinds of grain mixed together with molasses soaked into it. I have to be careful to eat breakfast before I go to feed the horses. Otherwise, I might be tempted to muzzle a little down myself; it smells so good!

Hey Girl had taken to standing where she could watch for me to leave the house to come feed her. The most advantageous spot was on a steeply sloping patch of ground. I stepped out the back door and called to her. Her mind must have been far off. She was so startled and excited that she took off in the direction of the stable and her food without regard to the steepness of the ground underfoot. She took one step, and because the ground was not where she had anticipated, she fell over like a potted tree in a windstorm.

Being on the side of a steep hill, she disappeared completely from view! I ran over to the fence in time to see her get up and shake herself off. She still came to eat, but ambled over to the trough more slowly than usual as if her dignity had been wounded.

I once knew a very proud man who did the same thing. He was a man who hungered after respect from other people.

At a church outing one spring, he was standing with his hands in his pockets with his toes right up against a big oak tree root. He started to take a step forward but his foot was unable to move. He fell over with twenty pairs of fascinated, but helpless, eyes riveted to his in-slow-motion fall. He struggled for a moment to get his hands out of his pockets, then hesitated, apparently too long, and fell straightforward. He stuck his chest out, at least, and his face hardly touched the ground. He was the kind of man who hated sympathy of any kind and it must have been torture for him to have so many people fussing all around him. He wasn't hurt, but I don't think he was ever the same again either.

We have to be careful where we put our feet when it comes to being around things that stimulate our appetite—not just our appetite for food but our appetite for recognition and social esteem. *Pride [goeth] before destruction, and a haughty spirit before a fall* (Proverbs 16:18).

"Num Num Num!"

If horses could talk they'd say, "Num num num," in a musical way like my younger daughter would when she'd want a bite of her poor, never able to eat a meal in peace, mother's food. She would intone, "I want some!" not able to speak the actual words yet. What she lacked in vocabulary and pronunciation she made up for by pounding her little fists on the high-chair feeding tray, her little eyes looking questioning, hurt and demanding.

I think that's what my horses would say if they could talk. If they're in the upper field when I call out for them to come get some food, they run down to the fence nearest me, instead of along the fence line and around the house to the lean-to where I keep the food and where I am waiting to feed them. They look at me longingly as I'm pouring the grain, the molasses smell wafting through the air. They'd probably call out " Num num num!" if they could. Fidgeting back and forth, their hunger drives their compulsion to edge closer to the barbed wire. Finally, slowly, as if responding to some far-off distant siren call, they drift away along the fence line. At first they walk nonchalantly and slowly around the corner of the house. As they come around the other side, they are in a trot; by the time they approach the feeding shed they are racing each other at a gallop.

Silly creatures! How much the same we must look to God as he offers us a land full of milk and honey while we linger in the desert of our personal rebellion, trying to get satisfaction and sustenance *our* way. Yet somewhere in the back of our minds we remember that our way has never panned out and we turn again towards our Provider. *O taste and see that the LORD is good: blessed is the man that trusteth in Him* (Psalm 34:8).

Whispers in the Wind

I have two-inch solid foam insulation between my floor joists and I get a kick out of thinking how I'm keeping the heat from leaking out. I have the same sort of feeling when I buy a decent pair of shoes from *Ross-Dress-for-Less* after they have been marked down again. It's common sense to want to spend less money on the things you need.

The other night as I laid down in bed I felt like I was getting sick. The air felt too close and I couldn't breathe well. I tossed and turned. I thought maybe I was getting a fever. Finally, I reached over to open the window near the head of my bed an inch or two. As I did, a flood of wellness flowed over my senses. The fresh, cool air was delicious!

Sometimes I need to be less concerned about keeping in the warmth, less concerned about conserving energy or saving money, and more concerned about letting in some fresh air. Getting fresh air is a strong part of good health.

It has occurred to me that some people have the same

effect on me. They are like a breath of fresh air. They make me glad to breathe and glad to be alive and being around them adds to my sense of wellbeing. Young or old, it doesn't matter; it's their... their *essence* that seems to revitalize those around them. The French call it *élan vital*, the vital essence. It's available to all of us. We have to open up the windows of our souls to let in the fresh air. The same Spirit that hovered over the face of the void and formless earth in response to the creative Word of God hovers all around us, looking for an opportunity to refresh us.

Letting go of defensive thoughts about ourselves as well as negative thoughts about others, which we sometimes put up to insulate ourselves against the cold world, is like opening the windows to our souls to let God's Spirit wash over us. *The wind bloweth where it listeth, and thou hearest the sound thereof, but canst not tell whence it cometh, and whither it goeth: so is every one that is born of the Spirit* (John 3:8).

No More Tears

My Dad is dying. We are keeping him home with us like we did Grandma Ella. She was 94 but sharp as a tack. Well, sharp as a tack that's been in constant use for 94 years.

She could understand everything; she just couldn't remember recent events. I remember how she kept asking, "Where's Garry?" while I was holding her hand, and how frustrated she felt when she realized what she was doing but was unable to stop herself.

These old bodies aren't made to last forever. God changed that when sin entered the world; He barred us from having access to the Tree of Eternal Life, so that sinfulness wouldn't last forever.

In the way of nature dead things decompose and provide nourishment for new life. Christ, having died on our behalf, gave His body to become the Bread of Life. The death of those we love can perhaps nourish our appreciation for this life, this life which the scriptures describe as grass that is here for a season and then dries up and is gone (Psalm 90:4-6). How precious is our time here and how short. Let us leave the worrying over the little things and the stressing over what is to come to those who do not have that better hope and to those who live as if there is no tomorrow. There is a tomorrow and a God who desires that it be rich and full. He permits sadness and grief over the things of today to go on a little while longer.

We know little of our tomorrows and even less about the land of eternal tomorrows, but we do know this—that the God who created us, loves us still and has a plan that will make it all worthwhile. With faith in Him and in His plan, life is worthwhile now. We can let our tears flow over the loss of our loved ones knowing that, in the end, God will wipe away every tear. *And God shall wipe away all tears from their eyes; and there shall be no more death, neither sorrow, nor crying, neither shall there be any more pain: for the former things are passed away* (Revelation 21:4).

Be Thou Our Vision Even in War

In times like these, when war and the rumors of war causes the pain of humanity to cry out to the heavens, we all need to focus on the vision of peace God reveals to us in the scriptures. We should remember God's plan does include a time of trouble, which will seem like a small ripple in the pool of eternity.

And yet, when we think of war and the swelling tide of human suffering, how can we be content now only with the peace God will unfold for us in the future? Paul writes how he has learned to be content in all situations. However, I am sure that his contentment allowed for the occasional shedding of tears over the pain and cruelty he must have witnessed in the harsh Roman world which eventually called for his execution.

Have whatever political opinions your best and prayerful reasoning affords, but please leave room for your heart to break over the pain of the Iraq and American families which have been devastated in this war.

Does God mourn less for a dead child because his skin is darker or the politics of his parents may be the product of ignorance and despotism? Do the angels feel less sad at the loneliness and despair of an elderly man whose only son was killed serving his country if the cause for which he fought was noble or right? Weep then at the loss of human life because it is of such amazing value that God, who created all things, gave His only Son to redeem it, and to save it from the suffering of sin and death. Be consoled that this same God will dry those very tears later and He will remember the compassion that flowed through your quickened heart during this sad time of war and terrorist strife. *...For I have learned, in whatsoever state I am, [therewith] to be content. I know both how to be abased, and I know how to abound: everywhere and in all things I am instructed both to be full and to be hungry, both to abound and to suffer need. I can do all things through Christ which strengtheneth me* (Phil 4:8b-13).

God's Plans, Not Ours!

When I moved away from Miranda to the Santa Rosa Area ten years ago, the first house we found was along the railroad tracks. It had a couple of dormer windows and a fireplace in the bedroom. We wanted it because it was so cute. I tried to make it happen, but, despite my best efforts, it just didn't work out. I learned later that the value of houses in that area suffered from being so close to the railroad tracks, which after a long time idleness were intended to be used again. The house we did move into turned out to be a wonderful experience, a solid investment, and a joyful home.

Four years after we moved to our present church assignment, my Conference re-districted my church and combined Rohnert Park with the Cloverdale church three cities away. The Conference President had computed it would be a creative solution, solving several problems. Some initially objected to the plan, including myself, because of the impracticality of the churches being situated so far apart with a number of other churches between them.

However, in a short time, it became obvious that the Lord intended a multitude of blessings in this arrangement. A wonderful rejuvenation of the church occurred, and my own life was profoundly blessed with meaningful friendships and spiritual growth.

Years later my Conference decided to district my present church in Fortuna with a congregation in Miranda I pastored years ago. I guess I'm maturing in the Lord because it didn't take me long to feel confident that the Lord will provide blessings to everyone concerned. Some are already obvious—the opportunity to renew relationships with beloved old friends, the opportunity to extend professional growth by taking on new challenges, and the ministry opportunities afforded to the local leadership to exercise their spiritual gifts for speaking and teaching.

Of one thing I am even more certain—God has a plan and it often doesn't revolve around our personal preferences! *"For I know the plans that I have for you,"* declares the Lord, *"plans to prosper you and not to harm you, plans to give you hope and a future...."* (Jeremiah 29:11).

Garry Genser

The First Shall Be Last

I want to call her "YooHoo," but since she is Suzanne's horse, who knows what she'll wind up being called. I like YooHoo because whatever you call a horse, you're going to wind up standing in front of your house and calling out her name loudly. Since I can't see myself with my hands cupped to the sides my mouth calling out, "Gertrude!" or "Alexandria's Inspiration!" I like names like "Hey Girl" and "YooHoo."

We said good-bye to Hey Girl's friend, the painted yearling we wintered at our place. We would have liked to buy him but his owner wanted more than was reasonable for our budget. It wasn't an easy good-bye because he had such a winning way about him. That night, Hey Girl whinnied frantically all night long. Horses are herd animals and, like people, are not meant to be alone.

It was only a couple of weeks until YooHoo arrived. Another rich sorrel mare with a white forehead and nose, she's a handsome horse with good manners and from the same practical and inexpensive breeder as Hey Girl. I expected Hey Girl to be thrilled. She responded, however,

41

as if she'd been starved for months and couldn't bear to have a single blade of her grass eaten by another horse. She'd race over to where YooHoo was grazing and demand again and again to stand and eat from exactly the same spot as the trespasser. All that green pasture, all those memories of being fed grain and alfalfa so faithfully, and here she was acting like she couldn't spare a grainy crumb!

People act the same way sometimes, even Christians. We want our churches to grow, but we don't want to give up anything. A pastor friend shared how a church member asked a visitor to move because he was sitting in HIS place in the pew! How many churches have a scarcity of places in which to sit? I'm proud of my church family because visitors and new members tell me that they are treated with warmth and graciousness. *But many [that are] first shall be last; and the last [shall be] first* (Matthew 19:30).

I Can Do It Myself

Echoes of my daughter, Dana's, childhood rang in the tone of her voice as she reminded me that she already knew how to ride, and reminded me how she had taken lessons for a full year as a child. I remembered. I had worked out an elaborate trade in order to encourage a family to return to our church school in Miranda—horseback-riding lessons from their oldest daughter for my two children in exchange for my paying part of their tuition. So Dana did know how to ride, but after all, it had been ten years since she had taken those lessons.

Reminding her on which side of the horse to mount, I watched her lead Hey Girl around the driveway. We were off for our ride. But, when Dana held her reins a little too tightly, telling Hey Girl, in effect, to go backwards, while at the same time kicking her heels in to tell her horse to go forward, Hey Girl naturally acted skittish. Dana got a little scared.

Being a courageous young woman, she didn't let it get the best of her. She pressed onward, but with more apprehension than enjoyment. If she had accepted a little more help, perhaps a few words of wisdom before she mounted, maybe she would have had more fun.

Having 27 more years of life experience than my daughter, you'd think I would have already learned how to accept help more comfortably than I do.

Recently, my little garden tractor broke down in my lower field and no matter how hard I tried, I just couldn't fix it. I have a friend with a four-wheel drive truck and another, who's an expert at fixing small engines, but I decided, rather than asking for help, I'd go get the tractor myself with my two-wheel truck. With the help of newly purchased ramps and a hand-held winch, I'd haul that tractor up on my truck and bring it into town to be fixed. Of course, my truck got stuck in the mud after a winter-full-of-rain had saturated the lower field.

So, after spending the money on these ramps, purchasing the winch, doing without my truck for months, and suffering from the accumulated garbage I would have been taking to the dump with the stuck truck, I had to ask the same guy with the four-wheel drive truck AND the friend who fixes small engines to help me. On top of that I of course had to have my friends observe my folly in the form of a truck and a tractor stuck in the mud.

Why is it so hard to ask for help? It's a funny sort of pride that makes us want to appear as if we don't need any help, and perhaps a little fear that we'd be turned down if we asked. Just think of all the wisdom that God has given to those around us and all the gifts he has given to friends and neighbors. How much more rich we all we would be if we learned not only to share what we have, but to ask for help at times, too. God expects us to work hard to help ourselves, but He wants us to live in a community of caring mutual interdependence too. *Bear ye one another's burdens, and so fulfill the law of Christ* (Galatians 6:2-3).

Fatal Flowers

It's the things you love that can save you or kill you. I love the beauty of the world God created. I love the mountains, the rivers, and most of all the people. I've heard people say that flowers are smiles from God. I love flowers.

Many years ago, following my love of nature, I stopped worshiping the Creator and fell in love with created things. I spent years wandering in the wilderness before beginning to see my need for Him.

Now, the beauty of the creation doesn't tempt me anymore to forget the Creator, but the flowers still kill me—not at first, but slowly, gradually.

First, I admire them in open wonder, gasping at the early spring explosions of lilies and storms of the acacias' yellow blooms. Then, the scotch broom laces the valley sides, framing the omnipresent mustard on the valley floor with even more bright yellow. In my awe and appreciation of all the beauty, I hardly notice the nagging tightness in my chest.

"Well, maybe it won't be such a bother this year," I

say to myself in a ritual I perform every year when I am reminded about my asthma.

Days later, I'm sucking on my inhaler all day long, but not until I'm up five or six times a night grasping for my inhaler do I give in and admit that I need to starting taking more medicines. The next bump up in treatment for asthma and allergies is the kind that takes time to build up in your system, only giving relief after a few days or a week. Not paying enough attention to my symptoms, I put off starting on the medications that I need so much and I wind up struggling for breath until they finally begin to take hold.

Sin is like that. It creeps up on us while we are appreciating the beauty of something. With wisdom, an asthmatic learns to tell the signs and starts taking the proper medication before his lungs get so inflamed that he's utterly miserable. With wisdom, we sinners learn the signs of temptation and make an appointment with the Great Physician before sin drags us so far down. God's medicine often takes time to work, so it's wise to get it before we are desperate. *But the wise took oil in their vessels with their lamps* (Matthew 25:4).

A Deadly Light

With my mind racing, I wondered how I could get a vet to come all the way out to Centerville Beach quickly enough to put YooHoo down before she suffered too much. She had thrown both her hind shoes in the horse trailer and had worked herself into a deadly panic. Making things worse, when I stopped, the trailer was at a slight decline toward the right side. Convinced she was going to die if she didn't get out of there, she kicked the escape door open. This little half door is designed for the loader to leave the compartment if necessary after leading the horse in by the head. This is safer than trying to squeeze by the horse's heavy hooves and back out the way you entered.

Kicking this escape door open, she stuck her front leg out! I bent it upward and placed it back inside. As I was trying to close the door, she kicked it open again violently, plunging her head out! She had stretched her halter rope enough to do this and now didn't have enough rope to allow her to maneuver her head back inside!

She had ridden in trailers many times without a problem. However, in the thickness of her animal mind, she was convinced that she had to get out of there now! Terrified and soaked in sweat, her hair looked frothy. Her eyes were wild with panic.

She was incapable of realizing that I knew what was safest for her. She wouldn't let me back her into what she perceived as a dark and dangerous place. She wanted to be in the light, which she saw as the only way out. In her small half of the two-horse trailer, she actually turned sideways. Now both her head and her front legs were sticking out of the half-height escape door, bucking and kicking, trying to get out into the light.

I made a quick decision. I hurriedly unclamped the rope from her halter. That way at least she would not break her neck or hang herself on the rope. She wildly kicked and scraped her 15 hands-high body through the dangerously narrow and short hatch, cutting and banging her ankles and legs against the metal door frame. After a torturously long thirty seconds, she was out. Although bleeding some from minor cuts on her thigh and both front legs, she was willing to let me walk her around in my efforts to calm her.

Her cuts were superficial; her sweat began to dry; her eyes lost that wild look; again she trusted herself to my care. After Suzanne and I washed her wounds, we were determined not to let this horrible event become our horse's phobia, ruining her from ever freely setting foot in a horse trailer again. So, we forced ourselves to load and unload both horses into the trailer, go for a ride then load them back into the trailer before returning home.

Sometimes we all feel afraid of the darkness of this world, especially when some traumatic event makes us frantic. One definition of sin is trying to get out of the darkness in a way that God has not designed for us. The alluring light is there, the promise of relief from pain perhaps, or relief from loneliness, boredom or anxiety. In our blindness, we go for it, not knowing, or for the moment not caring, about the deadly dangers. *For the wages of sin is death; but the gift of God is eternal life through Jesus Christ our Lord* (Romans 6:23). Thank God that *...when we confess our sins ... He is faithful and just to forgive us our sins, and to cleanse us from all unrighteousness* (1 John 1:9). Thank God that He is always willing to take us back into competent care, eventually transporting us safely home.

Following the Fallen

I would never have ridden down the beach stairs my-self, but my friend and horse mentor went down ahead of me without hesitation. I should have told Dennis, "No way!" but I was almost all the way down before I could see the washed-out last ten steps. My horse was too ner-vous to stand still for me long enough to dismount. It was too dangerous to linger on those steps, so I rode her back up to the stop of the stairs, dismounted and walked her back down slowly. When we reached the caved-in section near the bottom, we sidestepped off the stairs and made our own path down.

At the bottom I mounted quickly and looked for a path through the rivulets of tidewater streaming between the dunes and the ocean. YooHoo was ready to get mov-ing again. She didn't want to stand still. My friend prefers to bend the horse's will to his own in situations like this and kept giving instructions: "Loosen up on the reins!" "Neck rein her!" "Hold her with one hand, now." Though I complied with each instruction, it would have been easier for my horse to obey if she had sensed confidence in her rider or at least if she had sensed there was somewhere specific I was heading. But I was just trying to get her to stand still and she didn't feel comfortable just standing still there on the side of a dune.

Trying to quiet her down, I reined her in too tightly. She, wanting to be anywhere but on the dune, interpreted her reining to mean "back up," so she started backing up more quickly. Backing her up to a very steeply pitched sand dune near the embankment, with the sand caving in around each of her steps, she lost her balance and fell. My shoulder hit the embankment and I broke my scapula clean through.

It knocked air out of me that I hadn't known was there. My friend, not knowing I had broken my shoulder, thought we should keep on riding--you know, the proverbial getting right back on for your confidence's sake. He helped me up and gave my broken shoulder a vigorous rubbing.

I was willing to try anything by then, to stop the pain. I very slowly walked up the broad, sandy steps. It wasn't easy getting back up on the horse. Riding a mile or so convinced me something wasn't right inside. We rode up to a beautiful stone house in a nearby wealthy community. The pain on my face must have been plain to see because, instead of being frightened by two men on horseback at her front door, an incredibly kind and trusting lady who answered my friend's knocking insisted on driving me to the emergency room.

Vicodin and even morphine hardly touched the pain for the rest of the day. I now understand why the word, "exquisite" is an adjective sometimes used to describe a level of pain.

Maybe that's why God lets us have so much pain when we fall into sin... so we'll break free from following the lead of others and turn instead towards the One who only gives wise, safe counsel. We may follow others into confusion and sin, but only Christ's compassion can heal us from its wounds. *And the people, when they knew it, followed him: and he received them, and spake unto them of the kingdom of God, and healed them that had need of healing (Luke 9:11).*

Feeling Bats

I had heard the sound against my window screen before but was too sleepy to do anything about it. I was in the twilight of sleep where you hear things but don't attach much meaning to them, like someone saying something so mean-hearted or outrageous you don't even believe it until later.

Later in the night, minutes, or hours later according to my nonexistent inner clock, I heard the sound again, an annoyingly persistent deep fluttering of mothy wings. I reached out and almost squashed the dusty, bulky flying thing but only succeeded in knocking it down beside the dresser where it quieted down and settled in for the night.

The next night, while we were getting into bed, it crawled out from behind the dresser and flew around the room, looking like, and being in fact, much more of a bat than a moth. Suzanne screamed and shrieked like a little girl. She drew her blankets around her head to escape the bat, now circling the room to avoid my half-hearted attempts to hit it with a pillow. The air strikes were rather lame. I was forced to attack with my left arm, since my right one was still recovering from a broken shoulder. Realizing how revolting it would be to have my face, at some point in the future, against the same pillow I had used to kill a bat, my efforts became even more hesitant. You ever try to kill a bat left-handed and with watered down motivation?

Of course I wound up simply opening the sliding glass door and chasing the bat outside. Naturally, I was delighted to hear Suzanne shriek at something other than my past exploits with snakes and mice. (My juvenile pleasure in all this excitement, I must admit, is always slightly watered down afterwards by Suzanne getting a little mad. I have to remember at those times that in a year or two Suzanne would think it's funny too.) But, the thing I remember most vividly about our bat experience was how soft and furry that bat felt when I thought it was just a moth. I would NEVER want to feel a bat. I'd rather stick my hand in a plastic garbage bag that someone had spilled honey into. But not knowing the reality of what it was I was feeling, it didn't bother me at all.

Sin is like that. It doesn't feel bad; sometimes it even feels good, but only because we are ignorant of the repulsive reality under our fumbling fingers.

Feelings exist only as processed through our brains. Feelings.... We run our lives by them, even when they are produced by faulty assumptions. The next time you are tempted to do something driven only by your feelings remember how Esau lost his inheritance because while his body only said "hungry" his feelings said, "starving".

And Esau said to Jacob, Feed me, I pray thee, with that same red pottage; **for** *I am faint: therefore was his name called Edom. And Jacob said, Sell me this day thy birthright* (Gen. 25:30-31).

The Narrow Way

The measure of a good skier is his ability to turn. When I first learned to ski, I would build up speed to the point where I couldn't hold on to a turn. More often than not, this caused me to crash. There was always the not so elegant braking action of just sitting down, but that always ended up with me in a heap, sprawled all over the place.

Skilled turning is the key. When I learned to produce sharper turns, I could control my speed more easily—no more wide turns until I would be pointed slightly uphill to slow myself down! After I mastered this skill, I skied for a couple of years without hardly ever falling down. I remember the first time I made it all the way down a run without falling even once; it was so much more fun!

All worked well until a friend told me how a particular black diamond run wasn't really *that* hard. Foolishly trusting him, I discovered what he meant. It wasn't that hard for *him*! Much of the run was simply a logging road cut into the side of a steep decline. It was so narrow! I had to turn back and forth to keep myself from going too fast and there was so little room along the long, narrow, steep stretch. If I didn't turn sharply enough, I would wind up off the road either uphill to the left or downhill to the right. Uphill to the left would have been like running head-on into a door because of the rock face into which the road was cut. Downhill to the right meant a dramatic steep decline and certainly a visit to the orthopedic surgeon once someone found me. Not turning at all meant that I would build up so much speed that all hope of any control was lost. I was a danger to the other skiers. I fell so many times that by the time I made it down, forty-five minutes later, I couldn't ski for more than a couple of yards before my shaking legs would just give way. I was wrecked for the day.

Jesus said the way to heaven is narrow. We can't just wander in any direction and get there. We need to learn to turn at a moment's notice because scripture forecasts that the pace of our lives is going to increase; confusion as to what is right and wrong will abound. We need to become adept at not only keeping our eyes on Jesus but also on turning quickly when we find ourselves going in the wrong direction. There's no time to pretend it doesn't matter if we are going in the wrong direction; there's no time to defend a poor choice. As the speed picks up, we need to turn more sharply to correct our direction, or we'll wind up crashed on the rocks uphill or wrapped around a tree downhill. *Enter ye in at the strait gate: for wide is the gate, and broad is the way, that leadeth to destruction, and many there be which go in thereat: Because strait is the gate, and narrow is the way, which leadeth unto life, and few there be that find it* (Matthew 7:13-14).

Letting Your Feelings Flow

Animals don't seem having different feelings at different times. They simply feel what they feel based on their instincts and their circumstances.

But some people seem to want to feel the same way all the time. Now it's perfectly reasonable to want to avoid feeling pain and to seek good, pleasurable feelings; otherwise we might develop a habit of leaning on a hot stove or forgetting to eat, but I find within myself the tendency to want to feel good *all* the time.

I'm learning though, that it's okay to feel sad sometimes just because I do. The trick is to remember that nothing ever stays the same. Why worry when you feel a tad blue? Eventually the feeling will pass. Why long for those moments of exhilaration in life, as if they can be captured and made to stay? All things pass except the love of Jesus Christ. He experienced joy and anger, loneliness and sadness, accepting each passing feeling as if it was as natural as the cycle of a passing season.

Clinging to feelings of being young and attractive

can make the best of us appear a little silly. Needing to hang onto feelings of self-sufficiency can cause some elderly people to risk their own lives and the lives of their neighbors by driving long after they are safely able. A young man trying to hang onto days without care or responsibility can endanger his future, growing up to be a faithless husband or a non-contributing member of his church and community.

Letting go of a night's sleep and getting up in the morning to go to work results in the satisfaction of a day's work. Moments of sadness can clear the palette for the sweetness of tenderness and caring yet to come. And all the sorrow and trials of this life pave the way for the unfettered outpouring of God's love and the unobstructed glory of the re-creation of a world no longer darkened by sin. *When I was a child, I spake as a child, I understood as a child, I thought as a child: but when I became a man, I put away childish things* (1 Corinthians 13:11).

A Little Dirt Beneath the Surface

I had a row of young pines, each six or seven feet tall, on the wrong side of my driveway. If they matured, they would have joined with the much older and taller trees on the other side of the driveway. Their roots would have torn up my already mosaic driveway. They would have totally blocked out the sun and a beautiful view of the valley.

I chose to cut them down, myself, at a convenient height. My reasoning was based on my intention of later cutting the stumps a little below ground level where they'd eventually rot and disappear from view. After several weeks I tried to cut the stumps down, but the sap had started to rise. I couldn't cut more than one or two stumps without dulling a new chain on my chain saw. I was told it was probably because of the sap; however, when a more knowledgeable friend, Don, succeeded in cutting down the remaining ten or so stumps without dulling his saw, I found out what the problem really was.

Don took much more care than I had taken to clear

away the dirt clinging to the bark a couple of inches below ground level. Even though I had been clearing away almost all the dirt where we were trying to cut, I had been leaving small amounts clinging to the bark—not enough to notice much visually; just enough to dull the edge of the cutting chain.

Getting the sun to shine more brightly on the fields of our lives, we sometimes have to get rid of things that are otherwise pretty and even harmless— even things we like or that may have some value.   It's the little bit of dirt with which we fail to bother that sometimes can dull the edge of our spiritual sword. *If your ax is dull and loses it's edge, it's a lot harder to chop something down; trying harder helps but you really need to fix what is wrong* (Ecclesiastes 10:10, my translation).

Garden Walls

Between the thinly graveled parking area of my driveway and a cinder block retaining wall, holding back the hillside from the driveway, was a soggy, weedy area. Above the cinder block wall was another retaining wall, but this one was composed of garden brick. Being picky about visual things and being a self-proclaimed artsy person, this poorly designed area in front of my house bothered me. For the last year I imagined all sorts of different solutions. I finally settled on plans to build a third, really short retaining wall beneath the soggy area. I decided to construct this wall, as well as covering the exposed top portion of the cinder block wall, with garden bricks.

Great plan! I purchased the gravel and piled the earth needed to build up the boggy area. At this point I needed to rent a tractor but the piles of construction materials blocked the driveway where the rig, which would deliver the tractor, would unload and turn around. I didn't have a lot of time to figure it out because unless the garden bricks were in place before the first rain, the new lowest raised area would just wash away.

It got even more complicated. Unloading one of the piles of construction materials I bumped against an outdoor spigot and the flooding caused by the broken pipe was making the earth too soggy to support the tractor I needed to complete the job, unless I got an over-priced plumber to come on a double-time basis on a Sunday to repair the broken water pipe. The point was that everything seemed to depend on something else or someone else in order to go forward.

Do you feel that way at times, like everything is being held up, waiting on someone else to either make a decision or to do their work so you can go ahead with a task or a project?

All the tools and materials and skills needed to get this job done finally came into play and the work went forward. Now the area looks pretty attractive. There are even plants trailing over one retaining wall edge down to the next lower level. One piece of equipment missing or one task done out of order and the work would have ground to a halt.

What forward momentum in the lives of your family, friends, or community is being held up waiting for action on your part? What part of the building of God's kingdom is required of you and me for the work to move forward? *And whether one member suffers, all the members suffer with it; or one member be honored, all the members rejoice with it* (1 Corinthians 12:26).

Sharing Our Feed

Hey Girl is not a very friendly horse. She grudgingly nuzzles me when she realizes that the grain is going to stay in the bag unless she loosens up and gives a little affection. She clearly prefers food to affection. All horses prefer food to affection, but, for some, affection isn't so out-of-the-question.

YooHoo, for example, likes some company—mine, Suzanne's, other horses; she's just a social animal. She follows Hey Girl around in spite of the scars on her right rear thigh where Hey Girl's antisocial tendencies left their mark. Our neighbor's bay gelding might be emotionally scarred after the treatment he received from Hey Girl. He used poor judgment by jumping over the barbed wire fence to join Hey Girl and YooHoo. Hey Girl was friendly enough, apparently, to encourage the foolish act. Once the gelding was on Hey Girl's side of the fence, however, he began eating *her* grass and distracting YooHoo from giving her the continuous homage she expects. So, Hey Girl responded by showing the gelding just how extremely unwelcome he was. He was allowed to exist on the eastern side of the slope, but when he tried to follow the mares toward the feed trough at lunchtime, he was made to understand, in no uncertain terms, that lunch was by invitation only. Apparently it is one thing to be friendly to an overly eager neighbor across the fence, but it is another thing to be expected to eat with him. The poor dope— not only wasn't he welcome with the women-folk, but he was stuck because he couldn't figure out *how* he got on this side of the fence. I'm sure he already had forgotten *why*. My neighbor had to come over and cut the fence, get his horse back through it, and rewire it.

Hey Girl barely even puts up with YooHoo when it comes to sharing food. She flails out her rear leg from time to time, whacking the side of the feeding stable wall, just out of principle, even if YooHoo isn't nearby. During mealtimes YooHoo is just tolerated, being forced to stand with most of her body out in the rain while she's barely allowed to share the trough.

Sometimes we welcome new people into our churches, but then hold them at arm's length. Those new people who find themselves invited to three homes for a meal within six months or so are likely to hang in there and remain members. Those who are not welcomed into at least three homes are statistically more likely to look elsewhere for the fellowship everyone needs to thrive. *The wolf and the lamb shall feed together, and the lion shall eat straw like the bullock...* Isaiah 65:25. *Wherefore, my brethren, when ye come together to eat, tarry one for another* (1 Corinthians 11:33).

Hiding our Feelings

People do the strangest things sometimes and don't seem to bat an eyelash: I bat an eyelash and sometimes, strangely enough, worry about it for days. I recently shared with someone my irritation at some behavior on their part. What plagues me now isn't their misbehavior but that I allowed my irritation to show. Where did I get the idea that concealing my irritation was such a virtue? Why do I think that negative feelings should be hidden?

Animals don't hide their negative feelings. But then, you ask, what do they have to feel negative about? Standing around all day eating grass, for example, doesn't exactly justify being outraged at life. But when animals are scared, they run. When they are impatient, they stamp their hooves, if they have hooves. When they feel threatened they either run away or return the threat to ward off the aggressor. But do animals really get angry?

I think anger is a human thing. I don't think it's bad. Jesus felt anger. He snorted with anger when he heard the probably hired mourners, common in those days, at the funeral of His friend, Lazarus. He was at least a little riled when he overturned the money changers' tables in the courtyards of the temple. Jesus expressed anger but yet He never sinned. So we can express anger and not sin, though it is a trick.

Because we are so much more likely to sin while we are expressing anger, scripture tells us: *Be ye angry, and sin not: let not the sun go down upon your wrath* (Ephesians 4:26). Some people allow anger to control them or use anger to control others. We know that anger isn't the cure-all, ... *for the wrath of man worketh not the righteousness of God* (James 1:20).

Since anger has a place in our human nature, it follows that we shouldn't deny it or hide it. At the same time we shouldn't let it run rampant or even remain cooking on the burner over night. Ultimately, only God has the wisdom to balance all these issues in a healthy way that prevents us from justifying any nastiness or elevating our own viewpoint.

If we use the following scripture as a check, we can stop hiding our feelings, be more real with one another, and at the same time check that our motives are okay and that we are not letting self-righteousness rule. *Recompense to no man evil for evil. Provide things honest in the sight of all men* (Romans 12:17).

Treasured Moments

The gray swirling blanket of mist covers the lower hills in front of the southern ridge of the Van Duzen River Valley, exposing both the valley floor and the tree-lined ridge above. Some mornings there's a light gray blanket smoothed out from ridge to ridge with a glow from the eastern side, betraying sunlight that is about to break through.

On other days there's a solid gray wall, as if no sun exists in the heavens at all, and there is nothing to be seen—no fields below with the cows eating autumn's retired corn stalks, no trees standing starkly along the ridge. On these dark days the horses perking their ears in different directions, or the cattle moving about lazily across from the pumpkin patch, are equally hidden from view. And yet, sooner or later, the sun does come out melting the gloom. Vivid field greens and bright sky blues peer through the fog revealing a river valley panoramic.

For moments only, or perhaps forever in the mind of the beholder, the dew glistens on the blade of grass, fragile and temporary. How precious is each passing moment when we glimpse the beauty of God's world. *Remember now thy Creator in the days of thy youth, while the evil days come not, nor the years draw nigh, when thou shalt say, I have no pleasure in them* (Ecclesiastes 12:1).

Broken Bones and Kept Promises

"Do you have any anti-inflammatories I could borrow?" I yelled out from the back of the long flatbed trailer half full of port a-potties. Eventually one kind camper lady gave me a couple of Advil, and I ran to catch up to the Junior Division crew. Not helping my crew to pick up the port a-potties after Redwood Camp Meeting because my shoulder hurt would be the equivalent of social suicide. The ribbing and ridiculing would be unbearable, especially when directed at me, their leader, and at 50 the oldest person of the crew, a person who had a secret agenda of proving that he was not really growing as old as he really was.

It wasn't too much later, about seven years ago, that my shoulder started making popcorn-popping sounds when I worked out. I have spent most of my life finding excuses not to work out, so I chose to disregard my alarm and the pain as mere rationalizations to stop exercising. I thought I'd just work through the pain and by building my shoulder muscles up even more I'd overcome the problem. More weight, more repetitions led to more pain. Finally, other guys at the gym who were a few feet away would look startled when they'd hear my shoulder making these grinding, clicking sounds. Being particularly stubborn, I kept lifting weights until my shoulder completely gave out and I tore a ligament.

I resisted surgery, hoping rest would cure it, until it got so bad that I couldn't even tuck in my shirt or close a car door without sharp pain. Arthroscopic surgery worked wonders. I was swinging a hammer on home projects while my arm was still in a sling. I'm no wimp!

A couple of years later my horse lost her balance on a steep sand dune and fell down on me. I couldn't hear my shoulder bone break, but I knew something was wrong. Of course I had to get right back on the horse because of the weight of proverbial wisdom, but I gave up after a couple of miles and was driven to the emergency room. The X-ray technician wasn't allowed to inform me what he saw on the X-rays but said, "Don't move your shoulder until you see the doctor!" And of course it was all in the same shoulder I injured just a few years before.

I healed up just fine and was pain free until I built some retaining walls. I guess you use certain muscles and put pressure on little-used tendons when you do a lot of repetitive movements, like laying several hundred landscaping blocks. Now, I can't reach out to pick up a glass of water without it hurting.

Folk wisdom says, "If you don't use it, you lose it," but scripture says we have been given only a certain amount of years (Job 14:1). Anyone who has ever owned a car knows that things wear out. So do our bodies, whether we like it or not. I admire and hope to become like those stoic souls among us who face the later years of their lives with such good humor. Aging bones may be more easily broken, but God's promises are not. It may not make a sore muscle feel better, but God's promises do help us to accept our limitations and to look forward to a time when our body parts won't wear out and need replacing like an old Volvo.

In a moment, in the twinkling of an eye, at the last trump: for the trumpet shall sound, and the dead shall be raised incorruptible, and we shall be changed. For this corruptible must put on incorruption, and this mortal must put on immortality. So when this corruptible shall have put on incorruption, and this mortal shall have put on immortality, then shall be brought to pass the saying that is written, Death is swallowed up in victory (1 Corinthians 15: 51-54).

Christmas Family

Christmas time is a family time. We all yearn for the warmth and tender comfort of family love. The child in me will miss my Mom and my Dad who are both gone now. Our own children's work schedules prevent them from coming home this year for Christmas, so we'll go down to San Francisco to spend the day with them.

So many people have experienced grandparents, parents or, even more tragically, children who have passed away. Some may have family members who are serving overseas or unable to be with them for other reasons. We know that in heaven there will no longer be any death and all our tears will be wiped away, but God has planned for fulfilling our needs and healing our deepest wounds *now*.

He has given us a new life complete with a new family now. That's what God intends for Christians through the blessings of a local church family. He wants us to be a heavenly family to one another. Suzanne and I are so grateful for our church here in Fortuna, where we have been so welcomed and accepted. There are those here, and most likely in every church, whose encouraging smile are like a father or mother. There are others whose comradeship and willingness to help are like that of a brother or a sister. And there are the children who are like everyone's children, ready to laugh and to learn.

Some of you reading this may have fallen into a false sense of not needing a family or fallen into the untrue sense of not being needed. Your needs, at one time or another may not have been met because of some unloving event or unkind person, but a family is not defined by the evil that may be in it. Not until the church is glorified will all evil be purged. I am so sorry that someone may have hurt you or that you or your loved ones may have had needs or hurts that were neglected. I am sorry that church leaders, now or in the past, may not have been sensitive enough to know how or when we might have been able to help you. Or perhaps you have spiritual gifts that go unnoticed and you are feeling unappreciated. Please don't let Satan take advantage of the faults or sins of others and use discouragement to separate you from the love that is available to you through God's family. Weak and imperfect as it is, God's Church is the object of His supreme regard.

The truth is, you can't really make it very easily on your own. Perhaps it is in dealing with the imperfect bunch of people in the church that your greatest blessing may be lacking. Learning to forgive others for their sometimes hurtful ways, learning to love others who may not at times seem very lovable, learning to let yourself be loved by people who may seem beneath or above you, similar to you, or very strange and hard to understand, that is what spiritual growth is all about. Without all the pain and sometimes comfort, without all the loving and letting yourselves be loved, without all the frustration of making decisions together when we all think so differently, there would be no opportunity for growth; that is the stuff of spiritual life and without it a part of us dies.

Give God a chance again and join or rejoin a church family—if not where you had been attending, then somewhere else. God's family is an extended family circling the globe. Come back to your brothers and sisters. Give them and give yourself another chance at love. *For as we have many members in one body, and all members have not the same office: So we, being many, are one body in Christ, and every one members one of another* (Romans 12:4-5).

Painting Over Things

We thought we would have grown to like the spongy, blotchy, artsy-craftsy paint job we did on our living room walls. We should have taken a hint that it wasn't going to work out when one visiting friend commented, "You aren't going to leave it like this, are you?"

The previous owner had a "paint it all glossy off-white so we can wash it after the next tenants move out" mentality, so we were anxious to add some color. We liked the color of the family room in our last house, and we have always liked keeping some things similar in our moving from-town-to-town minister's lifestyle. We decided on the same sand-washed textured green as we had in our last house.

Painting over the enamel and then blotting the walls with towels or crunched up newspapers produced a different effect than we had in our last house, though. A lot more of the off-white enamel color showed through. It looked... very different. Having a lot to do, and painting not being our most favorite pastime, we tried to learn to like it. We did a lot of, "It's an interesting look, don't you think?" and "It looks kind of like Southwestern stucco, huh?" to each other. In the end we decided it just looked like a too-thin layer of paint over an inhospitable too-shiny undersurface.

We finally painting the room a second coat on New Year's Eve. It's less unique but easier to look at now. It's funny how much time we can spend on making things look good on the outside. Sometimes we care more about what things look like than we do about how they actually are. As far as walls go, as long as they are strong enough not to fall down and to keep out the cold, it's all pretty much the same. But as far as our personhood goes, what looks good on the outside doesn't count for much in the long run. The people whose opinion really matters can usually see through the surface paint anyway, and, as far as God goes, He cares more about the deeper beauty, which can light up an otherwise dim and foreboding world than he does the surface of our lives.

Woe unto you, scribes and Pharisees, hypocrites! For ye are like unto whited sepulchers, which indeed appear beautiful outward, but are within full of dead men's bones, and of all uncleanness (Matthew 23:27).

One Foot in the Muck

Four months of rain plus fertile bottomland equals muck. My loafers weren't designed for traipsing around an alluvial plain, but I wasn't intending to venture out any further than the shed where I store my hay. After feeding the horses, the pleasant morning sun on my face caught my attention and drew me out from under the trees to the upper pasture along my driveway. Looking around at the beautiful spring grass, brilliant green but not prolific, like a two-day beard on a teenager's face, I noticed the absence of firewood left laying around from some pine trees I had cut down.

Who would steal *pine* firewood? Oak firewood I could imagine someone wanting to steal. Someone had gathered the small amount of wood I was going to give to a friend and carted it off to burn in their probably smoky hideout. Dirty tin cans probably litter the back porch where their too-skinny dogs sleep. Oh well, maybe the wood wasn't stolen but was misplaced somewhere, maybe in the same place as my one missing work shoe I use for painting.

Musing on these things, I found myself wandering around the place to check out what other mysteries might have occurred in my absence during all these months of rain. I noted the horses had made a new path around the blackberries to get at a little patch of grass in the southwestern corner. I couldn't help myself but had to follow the trail. I even crossed the seasonal stream created where the culvert leaves off without getting my feet wet. It wasn't so soggy down there after all. Encouraged, I spotted my garden mower, abandoned after the first heavy rain made it unlikely for it to make it up the hill. I started it to charge the battery even if I could not drive it back up. And with that, I headed out toward the center of the bottomland. I noted where I got the tractor stuck last winter. I noticed where I got my truck stuck while trying to pull out my stuck tractor. I remembered the spot where my friend burned out his clutch trying to pull my truck out of the mud that I had used to try to pull the stuck tractor. The next thing I knew my right foot sank into the mud and my shoe remained down in there after I pulled my foot out.

Unable to stop my forward momentum, I took another step, mushing my thin-stockinged foot into the mud. Staring at my shoe that was at the bottom of a muddy hole rapidly filling with water, I realized I had no better choice than simply slipping my foot down in there. Clenching my toes against the straining suction of the mud, I pulled it back up. Curiously, my foot now fit much more snugly and firmly in my shoe, rather like false teeth coated with Fixodent. My shoe didn't seem to want to come off any more. Once it warmed up in there, it wasn't even uncomfortable, though I would fall short of recommending it to someone with too large or loose-fitting shoes. I got so used to it that I forgot about it until I got back to the house.

The muck and filth of sin can get comfortable, and can even seem to be useful when we traipse around in the bottom-land of this world. God doesn't want us to avoid the fertile places where there is a harvest of souls to be had or to remain in our ivory towers where everything is clean and beautiful. He wants us to remain clean and pure even when we have business in the muck. *Wherefore take unto you the whole armor of God, that ye may be able to withstand in the evil day, and having done all, to stand. Stand therefore, having your loins girt about with truth, and having on the breastplate of righteousness; And your feet shod with the preparation of the gospel of peace* (Ephesians 6:13-15).

The Need for Friends

When I first brought Hey Girl home she wandered around, nervously looking the place over in shock at being cut off from her familiar herd. I left her alone for an hour or two and then walked up to the field above my house with Suzanne in tow, to show her our new horse. When Hey Girl saw me, she let out a worried whinny and trotted up very quickly to where I was standing and put her head close to mine, relieved to be with someone familiar. Suzanne thought it showed that Hey Girl liked me, but she's not the kind of horse that really *likes* anyone. She's a good ride and easy on the rein, but she doesn't really like anyone, especially someone who sits on her back and expects to be carted around.

Horses are herd animals like sheep and Christians. After creating Adam, God commented, "It is not good for man to be alone," and then He created Eve. That's when things really started to happen. That's when things get interesting for us too, when we break out of our isolation and seek out the company of others. Jesus did. He had the twelve special friends that He not only taught but also sought out for fellowship and support for His mission. Our nature cries out for this kind of fellowship and support.

We have so many choices between good ways to serve and meaningful ways to participate in service in our Christian freedom just like the first followers centuries ago of whom the Scriptures speak: *And they continued steadfastly in the apostles' doctrine and fellowship, and in breaking of bread, and in prayers* (Acts 2:42).

The Need for Renewal

Have you seen any of those makeover shows on TV? I've seen talk shows where they also do make overs. They show guests in everyday attire, then dress them all up and give them new hair-dos. The audience is so amazed at how much better the guests look. Then there's the *real* makeover using all kinds of plastic surgery, dental work, exercise, and last, but not least, a new wardrobe. After this metamorphosis the "caterpillar" crawls out of the end-of-the-show-cocoon revealing its beautiful new wings.

There are house and garden makeover shows where run-down or shabby houses are transformed into interesting and appealing homes before our very eyes. The popularity of these shows reveals how much delight people take in seeing things improved. After a number of years, churches need some making over, too. A year ago our church board formed various committees to make recommendations for how our church might receive some loving care. The last time our church family undertook a major face-lift was over a quarter of a century ago.

The work was done with such good workmanship and practicality that almost everyone remarks on how well everything has stood the test of time.

The years have come and gone and the need for a refurbishing seems to be generally accepted—but not by everyone. I remember when one small church I pastored was refurbished twelve years ago, the first time since being built as a school playroom and a temporary church sanctuary combined. The forty-year-old draperies served somewhat as a filter for the nearby heating system intake vents which turned the cream-colored fiberglass fabric a charcoal gray near the ceiling. The single light bulb hanging from a wire above the pulpit lit up the faded outline where a plaque with a scripture had once graced the wall. The church, after some drama in the decision-making process, rallied behind the project and the humble country church was beautified. During the dedication ceremony, while the conference president was being seated in the elder's chair, still slightly tacky from the new varnish, one dear soul could be heard saying in the overly loud voice used only by those who are hard-of-hearing, "I didn't see anything wrong with the way it was!"

We all have different perceptions as to how a church should look, but not everyone is equally blessed with the ability to contribute to such an undertaking. People vary in their skills, in time available for labor on the project, and in funds available to donate. God does not command us to participate in any refurbishment of any sanctuary. It is to be done in the attitude of a free-will offering. However, those who do not feel called upon to

contribute to church improvements should take care to
*…Let the work of this house of God alone; let the governor
of the Jews and the elders of the Jews build this house of God
in his place* (Ezra 6:7).

Charles Fort

In the early 70's, when I was nineteen years old I hitchhiked around Europe. You've heard of those books like <u>Europe on Three Dollars a Day</u>, (obviously many years out of print). I could have written a book on how to do it even cheaper, but no one would have believed me or necessarily have wanted to repeat my experiences! I earned a little money doing pen and ink portraits of people on the street and never ate in restaurants except for the ubiquitous cafe-au-lait.

I stayed wherever I could unroll my army surplus sleeping bag but sometimes splurged and stayed in a youth hostel. In Ireland, in County Cork near Kinsale, I stumbled upon an abandoned Irish castle-like fort called Charles Fort. Its sea wall was still intact, as well as the turreted cutouts for the long missing guns. It had a long, arched tunnel as a back entrance that an intruder would have to bend over to walk through, making it easier for some soldier long ago to defend with a sword. Near this tunnel was a tall still-intact, grass-roofed room. We guessed correctly it was a stable. To my delight, I discovered that the room stayed dry and I, along with about thirty other young travelers from all over the world, took advantage of the free lodging.

We slept in the stable, often with a big fire in the middle of the stone room. Irish fiddlers and folk singers from Kinsale would sometimes stop by to play for us. We laughed and told jokes. What we all had in common was our youth and our desire to seek out others our own age. It was fun, but it couldn't last. Someone has to work. Just recently I discovered that the government has taken over the place and turned it into a tourist attraction, with guides, schedules, and a tea shop in what had once been the stables and the exciting summer home of my youth.

Why do youth want to spend time with one another so much? Maybe it's for the same reason we all like being around young people. They are so alive with promise and with potential. Our Fortuna youth leaders have been in communication with the other churches in the area and are planning more opportunities for our youth to spend time with one another. I wonder how many years of wandering and searching I could have saved if Charles Fort had been a Christian place, if behind the fun and laughter there had been life-giving truth?

Christian churches should encourage their youth to find fellowship with one another and to offer this fellowship to their communities. It's important because youth *will* gather, whether under loving guidance or under the influence of wild impulses. It's safer if they gather under loving guidance! *And he went up from thence unto Bethel:*

and as he was going up by the way, there came forth little children out of the city, and mocked him, and said unto him, 'Go up, thou bald head; go up, thou bald head.' And he turned back, and looked on them, and cursed them in the name of the LORD. And there came forth two she bears out of the wood, and tare forty and two children of them (2 Kings 2:23-24).

So let's support our youth and cherish them so that we will remain a part of their lives and be able to offer them what guidance we may.

Better Vision of What's Coming

My driveway onto Highway 36 is near a sharp curve. We're getting used to craning our heads sharply to the right to see if traffic is coming. Since there is also fast traffic coming from the left, with another curve limiting how far down the road one can see, entering onto the highway from our driveway is not for timid drivers. Looking quickly from one direction to the other, you have to make a decision and commit to it. The old saying, "He who hesitates is lost," takes on renewed meaning when you drive out from our place.

I've been wanting to cut down some of the shrubs and scrubby trees to expand our view of the approaching traffic from our driveway entrance, but the work was either just too nasty for my soft hands, or I've always had other projects that were more important. But that was before Nicholas, a new friend of mine and of our church, came along with a "can-do" attitude and a good work ethic.

Hours of dirty, itchy hacking, sawing, and chewing through the berries and brush left a mountain of debris for several large burn piles. A lot of trash from the highway was exposed, too.

Expanding our vision of what is coming at us in life is a part of wise living. God's word has lots of information on what is going to happen to this world. It takes some work to clear the way to see prophecies clearly and some willingness to expose hidden junk and wrong attitudes, but it's worth it. I'm so glad I belong to a church that values the insight into what is coming that the Word has to offer. *The LORD of hosts hath sworn, saying, Surely as I have thought, so shall it come to pass; and as I have purposed, so shall it stand* (Isaiah 14:24).

Poison Oak

Poison oak is so aptly named. It has leaves that look a little like oak leaves, but it is poison. My daughter, Lara, is so allergic to it that her face will swell up till her eyes are narrow little slits. She gets like this even when she takes great pains never to touch the stuff. I'm so allergic to it that I break out in a rash just thinking about it.

Last week my friend Nicholas and I were trimming the branches overhanging my driveway and clearing out brush. There were times when my expert advice and strategic planning were not enough and I actually had to get my hands dirty! I had to venture out with him into the itchy stuff and do work I usually gladly pay others to do.

Carefully avoiding contact with anything remotely green is not easy when you are clearing brush. Unlike Nicholas who just had to scratch an itch on his neck, I was careful not to touch any part of my body with my hands that I just knew were contaminated with the nasty stuff.

Washing my hands carefully and washing my dirty

clothes, I thought I had a chance at not getting it very badly, but soon I started itching everywhere. When Suzanne came home from visiting relatives in Chicago, where I am pretty sure she had minimal exposure to poison oak, she immediately started itching. Since she didn't buy my explanation that maybe she got it on the airplane, I had to take responsibility, even though I couldn't understand how I could have contaminated her with the poisonous oil.

Days after, while I was putting on my shoes and tying my shoelaces, I realized what was happening. I must have re-contaminated my hands each time I tied my shoes, which had been in contact with the oily poison oak, spreading it to everything I touched until the next time I washed my hands.

That's why not even the slightest amount of sin is allowed in heaven. We must be willing to have every part of ourselves cleansed and to put on clean robes. Just a little is spread to everything we touch, and other people will suffer because of contact with us. Even now other people suffer for the little sins, which we may be willing to tolerate in our lives. Would we be complacent with these sins if we knew the full extent to which the poison travels? *A little leaven leaveneth the whole lump* (Galatians 5:9).

No Need for Speed

Soon after I got my very first car, a 1959 MG A, I visited a friend in Missouri. I took him for a ride and was showing off by driving way too fast on this section of highway that was under construction and not yet open for traffic. Since I didn't know the road, or rather how soon the road came to an end, I was still going very fast when the end-of-road barrier came into view. I hit the brakes and started skidding. The barrier was fast approaching and instinctively I turned the wheel sharply. The car was now going backwards and I put the car in first gear and gunned the engine.

The two forces started to neutralize one another as the tires eventually did more than just make smoke and they started to take hold. The car started going forward, in the other direction of the barrier. It all happened so fast I didn't have time to get scared and my friend, misinterpreting the nonplussed look I had on my face for confidence, said, "You sure know how to drive!".

I continued being a reckless driver although not a wreck-less one. My car, far from perfect when I got it, soon had evidence of my encounters with reality on all sides, except on the front bumper and the very classy little MG A grill. The Boston trip with my friend, John, took care of that. I was following him in a rainstorm. The rag-top was leaking profusely. The little toy-like windshield wipers were slapping the water around back and forth, making a kaleidoscope out of all the headlights shining in my face. The MG A rode very close to the ground, right at headlight level.

Driving most of the night, tired and blinded by the oncoming lights, I was unprepared when a truck passed me and bathed me in a wave of water that totally disoriented me. I slowed down as much as I was able and pulled over a bit too far onto the shoulder. A light post came into view, almost in slow motion, lit up by my headlights. My perfect front bumper and grill now had a slightly inwards design, where they were originally curved outward.

I remember what a hurry I was in as a youth now with amazement. It seems the less I knew where I was headed in life the more of a hurry I was to get there. *A wise man is cautious, but a fool is impulsive and reckless* (Proverbs 14:16, my translation).

The Birth of White Star

YooHoo had her baby, a healthy colt we named White Star because of the marking on his forehead. One day YooHoo was fat and pregnant, the next day, after a single excited whinny coming up from near the newly cleaned-out spring, she was a mother.

It was hard to get to her because Suzanne and I had to jump over the ditch we had dug to lay pipes to drain the spring. The stubble and sharply broken branches, remaining from the newly cleared-out berry bushes and brush, covered the slopes in front of her like the hair on a 15-year-old boy's chin. The prickly, crunchy debris from the newly cleared-out hillside looked so uncomfortable and inhospitable for the delicate, frail-looking baby horse picking its way between his mother's feet to peer out at us.

How could YooHoo pick such an unappealing place to have her colt? What if the baby stumbled and fell over the dangerous broken branches? Why didn't she have her baby on the soft, sweet-smelling carpet of growth down below near where the spring drains into the bottomland, or on the smooth, chewed-down grass a little higher? Or why didn't she choose to have him under the recently repaired stable roof where it would be dry?

When I asked a group of school children these questions, they figured it out instantly—to be safe from the approach of any enemies, from anything that would endanger the precious and fragile new creature.

It seems clear that God placed instincts within the mother to protect her baby from harm and those instincts drove her to find a place where enemies would either not see them or be heard approaching. Comfort was a low priority in the face of survival.

Have you ever wondered why God has allowed uncomfortable things into your environment? This world is nothing but a birthplace for the new hearts and minds that are being born in those who love God. Comfort is not a high priority in God's mind. His concern dwells more on our surviving the onslaughts of an enemy intent on destroying us. Part of loving God is to trust that He is able to control all things. What causes us discomfort may be part of a much bigger plan than we are able to perceive. *And we know that all things work together for good to them that love God, to them who are the called according to his purpose* (Romans 8:28).

The Death of YooHoo

YooHoo was fine one day and the next she was dead. Her baby, White Star, was sleeping next to her when I ran down to the lower field. I was alarmed at seeing them both lying there, not responding to my calling them for feeding. Colts can sleep very soundly and aren't roused as much by touching as they are by noises. My frantically shaking him and lifting his head up didn't immediately wake him. After a moment he shook himself and jumped up, resumed what he must have been doing for hours, nuzzling and nudging his unmoving mother.

I got a vet to come over right away, not for YooHoo; she was gone. The vet and I pushed and pulled White Star up to my horse trailer where we confined him. Otherwise he would just return pathetically to his mother's side. Once in the horse trailer I tried to get him to nurse on some formula Suzanne had already gotten from Fortuna Feed. It didn't go well.

The vet told me that this was really our only option because horses won't take on orphans. With formula splashed all over myself, and White Star totally stressed in the cramped and smelly steel trailer, I wasn't prepared to hear that I'd have to do this every couple of hours, day and night, for months.

Then Dennis, my horse rancher friend, showed up. He had said he couldn't come until the next morning, but after thinking about it, and remembering how hard it was when he had a foal's mother die, realized he needed to come help right away. The first thing he wanted to do was to move the colt to a shady spot behind my house. I told him that moving the colt unnecessarily would be way too stressful on all of us. He replied, "Naw, we'll just mosey him along right over." He showed me how to position myself so that I could wedge the colt with my hips. Then if the colt kicked, his feet would miss my shins. Dennis steered him with a foal halter while I pushed. The colt practically walked himself to where we wanted him. With the vet's method, all the wrestling around had been exhausting.

Dennis, growing up on a ranch and raising horses full time all his life, talked over the different options with the vet who hadn't left yet. Soon I realized that the young, very educated, and professional vet was listening attentively to Dennis. Within minutes Dennis had White Star feeding off a fidgety Hey Girl, along with her own colt. The vet was amazed, Suzanne was relieved, and I was in shock at the techniques involved in getting the colt tricked into trying out his new foster mother. You don't want to know.

To insure ongoing feedings would be better Dennis built a temporary pen to keep the two colts together so they would begin to smell more alike, convincing the mother to accept the orphan without having to be tied up. All the wisdom of the vet with all her education didn't save the colt. It took someone with the experience of actually having lived through the ordeal.

The world has lots of advice to offer on how to survive in this world of sin and death but only Christ has experienced this life and the darkness of death. Only He can save us. *But we see Jesus, who was made a little lower than the angels for the suffering of death, crowned with glory and honour; that he by the grace of God should taste death for every man* (Hebrews 2:9).

Death Is Not the Worst Thing

Sadder even than the sudden death of YooHoo was the fate of Hey Girl's baby colt, named Survivor because he had survived breaking through a temporary fence and falling into a cistern. He struggled to survive but could not recover from a broken jaw. He was able to suck and grow and even seemed strong and happy at times. He would run for no reason and buck up both his back legs and run back to his mother. He would play a game with me where I would rub his shoulders and chest vigorously until he would get overwhelmed and start to back away. As soon as I stopped rubbing, he would quickly take a step forward to ask for more.

My horse-rancher friend thought that maybe the jaw would set and the vet agreed that surgery wasn't a good option. It seemed, by how happy the colt was, that this approach was hopeful, but the broken jaw and surrounding damaged tissues, being so exposed and constantly irritated and drenched in milk, became infected. Eventually, x-rays and another visit by the vet confirmed that the bones themselves were infected and would never heal.

We put him down because there was no hope for a future without too much pain. I kept thinking of our little game and how he would step forward to be rubbed more. He and I would no longer have that little joy and pleasure again, but the important thing to remember was that he would no longer have the pain and suffering which he bore so silently and that would increase as the infection spread.

As much as I loved that little colt, there came a time when I would accept his death rather than have him suffer any longer. Christians sometimes suffer from questions over how a loving God could have allowed and even commanded for death to be visited upon some depraved and morally sick tribes recorded in the Old Testament. Some Christians even question how a loving God could allow for the destruction of the wicked on that final day when judgment is proclaimed. Isn't it clear that God would prefer the death of those He loved before he would allow for the misery and suffering of diseased humanity to continue forever?

Then death and Hades were thrown into the lake of fire. The lake of fire is the second death (Rev. 20:13-14). It is not just people who have rejected God who are mercifully put down. It's death and dying itself that's thrown into the lake of fire. It is a permanent end to sickness and suffering—forever! *And God shall wipe away all tears from their eyes; and there shall be no more death, neither sorrow, nor crying, neither shall there be any more pain: for the former things are passed away. And he that sat upon the throne said, Behold, I make all things new. And he said unto me, Write: for these words are true and faithful* (Rev. 4-5a.)

Comparing Ourselves

Generally, it is a bad idea to compare ourselves with other people. Either we come out on top in the comparison and have cause to feel pride, or we come out poorly in the comparison and then have reason to envy others or feel bad about ourselves. However, there are times when comparing ourselves can increase our view of what possibilities exist.

For example, other people, at times, demonstrate God's grace in such a wonderful way. Noting and appreciating their giftedness can cause us to ask for the same grace to be manifested in our lives. God loves to give good gifts.

However, wanting things that are particular to other people, like personality traits or physical attributes or things they own, is another matter. Wanting those things is really just coveting. Nothing good comes out of coveting. Coveting, like all sin, leads to unhappiness and is an even quicker route to a diminished sense of self worth than many other types of sin. It leads to lower self worth because it makes us unhappy with whom God made us to be and out of touch with the things God has planned for us; exploring God's plans for us always leads to a greater sense of self worth which has nothing to do with pride. Wanting some good gift you see in the lives of those we admire and praying a prayer of faith, which always includes a desire to surrender to God's will and His plan for our lives, never has this negative effect.

Comparing ourselves to others can lead to competitiveness, wanting to be more than other people or above them. Appreciating the gifts of others and seeking similar blessings from God can expand our notions of how good God is and how excellent are His gifts. *But covet earnestly the best gifts: and yet shew I unto you a more excellent way* (I Corinthians 12:31).

Camp Meeting

Camp meeting has come and gone again. Does your church have retreats or camp outs where you have a chance to focus on spiritual things as God directed His people to do in Old Testament times?

Over the years I have seen people enthused and excited during camp meeting only to lose their "high" when they return home. Sometimes I have even seen people discourage others when they get back because they expect the same level of excitement to exist in their home church as in the large camp meeting where speakers and musicians are often sought out from all over the world and friends and families gather from far away.

Excitement and joy can be from the world or from God. The more we are rooted in Christ the more stable are our moods and feelings. We can have many friends around us, or few, and our joy doesn't fluctuate. We can appreciate great music programs and yet still enjoy the more humble offerings of a local church because the Holy Spirit gives us an inward harmony which tunes our spirit.

As wonderful as camp meetings are, it is our daily walk with God which determines the course of our character development and influences how valuable our service to the Lord will be. So don't let the "after camp meeting letdown" get you down. Instead get down on your knees and pray that the inspiration you received will deepen your relationship with Christ for eternity. This is just as true with all the high points in your life. Let all your exciting memories enrich your spirit and deepen your commitment to seek Him!

.... And the ransomed of the LORD shall return, and come to Zion with songs and everlasting joy upon their heads: they shall obtain joy and gladness, and sorrow and sighing shall flee away (Isaiah 35:10).

Sweating Palms and Healing Hands.

When I lifted up my hands from the restaurant man-
ager's shiny desktop, I saw two revealing, sweaty hand-
prints. He noticed my glance and I watched his eyes
lower and I observed his double-take at the evidence at
just how nervous I was.

I needed the job badly. I had one more year to go
before I would finish college, that golden horizon just
beyond which lay all the wealth, new cars, endless funds
for hobbies, that first starter home, in fact the basis for
my future financial empire. At times I stressed over how
I would have the time to enjoy the country house and
my city condo, how I would have to learn to fly so that
I would be able to get from one to the other quickly.
There was so much to obtain, so much to enjoy. The two
sweaty palm prints gave it all away.

It was twelve years later when a different pair of hands
imprinted on my soul the lasting lesson that I had it all
wrong. All the plans for my future had really just been
a lifestyle dream built from my earliest childhood that
my happiness would begin when I... You can fill in the

blank from there.

When I... finished the fort I was building in the woods next to my house. When I... fixed the old television set a neighbor had given me. When I... saved enough to hitchhike through Europe. When I... published my first novel. When I... got married. The list was endless.

I was very stressed for such a young adult. I carried my stress in my neck maybe like the Israelites whom God called "a stiff-necked" people. My neck would get so stiff I would lay on my back with my head over the edge of the bed trying to stretch it out and force it to relax. Nothing I would do would give it much relief. My not drinking coffee didn't help but then who knows how bad it could have gotten if I did.

Sitting up in bed, hurting and praying about a multitude of things I had a holy experience I never shared publicly for fear of being thought too spiritually eccentric. While I prayed I felt hands being placed on my neck and the warmth, and healing which flowed from them brings tears to my eyes this day.

I don't understand why God chose to do this for me. I stopped worrying about things like I used to. I still may have a rare headache or stiff shoulders like anyone else but I have never had that debilitating and constant pain since. I have been led from the sweaty palm prints on my employer's desk to the forever-cherished healing hands of Heaven. ...*they shall lay hands on the sick, and they shall recover* (Mark 16:18b).

Meaningful Fellowship

Recently, I've heard some beautiful things about my local church family. One man visited our church a few years ago and was so impressed by the loving atmosphere he found here that he wanted from then on to move back into the area someday. About six months ago he had a job opportunity and moved here. It was a major turning point in his life, and he made some significant lifestyle changes. He has relocated for an employment opportunity now, but I expect that the love he experienced here for a number of months will have a major influence for the rest of his life.

Another young man, Joshua George, visited our church a number of months ago—the first time he had set foot in a church for many years. The experience was so positive he continued visiting local churches until he found one where he felt needed and stayed with it. This hungry student appreciated the weekly pot lucks there too! I invited him to preach in Fortuna recently and he shared his testimony. He found such a gracious reception and loving atmosphere that the experience affirmed his resolve to return to serving the God of his youth, and he is now planning to enter the ministry.

Apparently, how we treat people, especially in the short time we are in our church buildings, has a tremendous impact on people's lives. Imagine the power of God's love that could reach out to people if we expanded our fellowship outside the building as well. Most communities have small study groups or prayer fellowships. Can I encourage you to fellowship with some like-minded believers in your area? It's not only about what blessings will be available for you there it is also about how God can use you to bless others! *But if we walk in the light, as He is in the light, we have fellowship with one another, and the blood of Jesus, his Son, purifies us from all sin* (I John 1:7).

Prayer

One box had a kimono my daughter wore for a school play eight years ago, a black female undergarment, and a white table fan. I'm not sure what this implies about my wife's frame of mind when she packed it a couple of years ago when we moved. Should that box go in the painting shed with Suzanne's school-teaching stuff or in the garage? That box was just one of a whole shed full of stuff my friend Scott Rush and I were sorting out. A woven rope hanging patio chair from Mexico, cross-country skis, and an unpublished novel came next—boxes and boxes.

I started giving Scott stuff that he could use: an almost antique video camera, a small tent, and an old bicycle. I made mental notes of what I could give to Community Services and to the next Fortuna Junior Academy rummage sale. That still left lots and lots of stuff that threatened to clutter my newly cleaned out garage and pump-shed. Fatigue came over me, and I seriously considered just driving straight to the dump while the truck was still mostly full. It just wasn't reasonable to throw it all away. And yet it seemed so hopeless to be clutter-ing up the garage and shed, that I had just spent the day before cleaning out, with stuff from another place I was cleaning out today. I was so unmotivated I could hardly bring myself to lift a box.

"Why don't we pray?" Scott suggested. "Why *don't* we," I thought? We bowed our heads and soon God lift-ed me above my foggy and funky mood. I felt like the sun had come out on a February morning in Humboldt County. A very short time later the job was done.

Light is sown for the righteous, and gladness for the up-right in heart (Psalm 97:11). Sometimes, all we have to do is ask.

How Much Is Enough?

When I was close to graduating from college with a teaching credential I was faced with the prospect of getting paid to go to school instead of paying to go to school. The reversal of fortune was exciting and the possibilities seemed endless. Instead of the tiny trailer I was living in, I could get married to Suzanne and buy a tiny house which seemed like a luxurious mansion. The overgrown, beer-bottle-strewn patch of weeds was to me a verdant lawn with Eden-like flowers waiting to be called forth. I saw Suzanne start to cry quietly when I brought her through the front door, even though she tried to hide her tears. So we had our first home.

The poorest neighborhood in the town just meant there was no place to go but up. And up we went, but sometimes down. The tax revolt of 1979 eliminated my new teaching position and the recession of 1981 with its 18 percent interest rate mortgages slowed us down in my next ill-chosen career of selling real estate, but we always had a sense of being able to survive and prosper by hard work. We did survive.

After many years of having no health insurance, I remember how amazed I was after I had medical coverage at the idea of going to a doctor with less than a life-threatening injury or a debilitating sickness. As a child I rarely saw a doctor or nurse unless I had to be carried in.

It wasn't until I grew old enough to wonder if "middle aged" was still an accurate description (it is, I suppose, if I live to be a hundred and four), that I began to think in terms of *security*. Prior to this *I* was my security. I would do whatever was needed in order to get by and to care for my family's needs. Whatever it took, however humbly we needed to live, I would make it work.

But as I grew more… mature, I began to understand that I was a part of a process that hitherto I always thought was reserved for others—aging. Then came the thought that there would come a time when I would eventually need to retire and leave preaching to younger folks who would be more likely to remember what they were talking about at any given moment. The point is eventually I would have to retire and rely on retirement plans, savings, and the like. I wouldn't be able to rely on *myself* anymore, on my strength and ability to provide.

And since that realization, I have been forced to ask how much is enough? Do I need enough savings so that I can travel, enough to keep feeding my horses, enough so that I wouldn't have to worry about health expenses and emergencies? How much *is* enough?

Do we need enough at retirement so that we can continue spending at whatever level we have been used to? Well, if we have been saving for retirement then, at retirement, we should be able to at least save *that* expense! So surely, *some* things will be different. Most people advise to have a house paid off at retirement, so that should save the expense of a mortgage payment or rent.

But how much do we need for all the unexpected things, all the surprises life has to offer? How much do we need so that if we are not working we will be able to afford to be active and generous to our family and church?

My grandmother and grandfather were in their prime during the Great Depression. Everything was for sale and no one had any money to buy! People who had a job were lucky and considered prosperous. My Grandmother was abandoned by her first husband and had to bring up my mother all alone. She worked in a factory sewing gloves. She worked for thirty-five years sewing gloves. She remarried later, to a butcher. They lived for forty years in an attic apartment in Chicago until it was condemned and then they moved across the street to another attic apartment. This was before anyone cared about insulation. Those attics did not just get hot in the summer; they smelled of the city heat, a certain old building smell to which only city-dwellers can relate.

They had an arrangement that neither could spend any money without severe retribution from the other. When I would go visit them my grandmother would sneak me a five-dollar bill when my grandfather wasn't looking. She'd have a look of panic on her face that he might come in and see her philandering their money away.

They saved every penny they could. They never owned

a car or bought new clothes or furniture. My grandfather had a stomachache the year after he retired. He took an afternoon nap and never woke up. My grandmother found little stashes of money he hid from her all over the apartment. She was so angry.

She continued to live in that attic apartment for another year until she moved in with my father so she could save money. She couldn't bring herself to break her habit of saving but would just look wide-eyed and speak in a whisper about how much things cost these days when the subject of spending would come up. She had to be dragged to a doctor when she was sick because of how much they might charge her, even though she had insurance.

She lived till she was ninety-four. When her health was failing I remember once, when the subject of money came up, how she had a look of disgust on her face, and she said in her broken English, "Who cares about that anymore?"

I suspect in that final moment, no one really does.

I hope that I have enough to be generous to those in need, to my church and to my family, but if I am not generous now what's to think I will be later. The more mature I become, and the more financially stable I strive to be, the more I realize that there really is no such thing as financial security in terms of the amount of money that can be had. The more one has, the more that can be lost. The more one relies on anything other than God, the more insecure one will be and the more truly impoverished.

.... The beloved of the LORD shall dwell in safety by him; and the Lord shall cover him all the day long, and he shall dwell between his shoulders (Deut 33:12).

A Slap in the Jaw

White Star probably isn't teething anymore, but he still chews on everything in order to get a feel for what it is. When it comes to my skin or clothes, however, he's going to have to find some other way. Horses' front teeth are made for cutting and tearing grass. His teeth come straight together then pass one another like scissors. As a horse gets older, his teeth come together more at an obtuse angle, the lower and upper teeth slanting outward more and more. I guess that's where the slang expression, "long in the tooth," meaning someone who is getting on in years, came from.

White Star communicates with his mouth, tasting, smelling, giving, and getting affection. He sometimes has wet teeth marks on his hips, evidence that he is getting a little too perky or disrespectful toward Hey Girl or YooHooTwo. When he was a day old, he nuzzled me for the first time. It felt so good, like a kiss from a newborn baby. A foal spends almost a year in its mother's womb, so when it is finally born, it can do things like that. It can even get up and run within hours of being born, so nuzzling is an easy thing for it to do. Biting or tearing skin is an easy thing for a horse to do, too.

I remember when he was only weeks old and Suzanne and I had to supervise his feeding with his foster mother after he had been orphaned. We would sit by him in lawn chairs and play with him when he had finished nursing . He was so fascinated by our clothes, by the different textures, of which he could never quite get the feel until he would take a little bite. I would lightly tap the underside of his jaw and sternly say "No!" and he would stop.

Now he is so big that I couldn't possibly play with him unless I had trained him to refrain from biting. I wouldn't be able to trust him. Last summer, my horse-raising friend, Dennis Mayo, had a horse run up behind him, and before he could turn around, the horse had bitten him on the shoulder and dragged him thirty feet. Dennis has so many rodeo and horse-breaking injuries that he couldn't really afford to have his good shoulder tied up.

White Star still likes to nuzzle me and to have me scratch his neck and chest. He begins to rub his mouth on my arm, opens his mouth a little bit and hesitates, closes his mouth a little and again hesitates. Sometimes he just starts to rub his teeth on me until my other hand comes up under his chin and reminds him not to bite. He doesn't act startled or hurt but almost reassured. "Oh, yeah, I remember. No teeth allowed." His instincts tell him teeth are okay to use. My hand tells him teeth are not allowed on humans.

We are born with tendencies to sin which will remain with us until we are given new bodies. And yet the New Life of the Spirit gives us the power to rise above our instincts. The law gives us the knowledge of what is not allowed and even provides the slap. It's only the Spirit, however, that empowers us to live spiritually. If you are having problems with your instincts, don't beat yourself up, don't slap yourself on your jaw thinking you can train yourself not to bite, but submit to the Master and His love. Let Him train you. *For the LORD is our judge, the LORD is our lawgiver, the LORD is our king; He will save us* (Isaiah 33:22). *My son, despise not the chastening of the LORD; neither be weary of his correction* (Proverbs 3:11).

The Electric Fence and the Mud of Sin

White Star has always come to me since he was a day old, so I was really saddened when he shied away from me at the fence line. He even started to put his foster mother, YooHooTwo, between himself and me. Most of all, I just *missed* him, missed rubbing the underside of his jaw along his neck. A young colt's hair is much softer than that of older horses, and now that his winter coat was fully in, it was very fluffy and fun to feel.

I know what started his shying away. It was the wet ground from the first winter storm of the year. The ground was saturated and the electric fence, which is just a single strand of half inch rope-like fabric with a pulsing current passing through it, was much more efficient because of the earth's greater conductivity when damp. Electric current pulses through the fence harmlessly and doesn't complete a circuit unless it touches the ground where the negative side of the charger is staked. The ground is a very efficient conductor of electricity, especially when damp. A current can actually travel over miles of fence line and deliver a shock grounded through all that earth.

Anyway, the ground was wetter than usual, and the fence was ready to deliver a shock. White Star came right up to me like he usually did. I leaned a little closer to the fence and just as my hand was rubbing his forehead, my thighs brushed against the fence. Thousands of volts (at very low amperage) were picked up and transferred through my body, along my arm into my hand and right onto his forehead. His body was grounded with all four feet into the negatively charged earth. We both jumped back wide-eyed.

I, however, understood what had happened, but he couldn't and so he stopped coming up to me out of fear of another shock. For weeks I felt the loss of his closeness. Finally, I stepped over the fence, sprightly I assure you, and stood in the muddy field, careless of my clean new shoes, careless of how the horses' heavy steps splashed a little muck against my pants. I stood very still. I stood quietly in the mud and manure, far away from the electric fence. White Star hesitantly approached. The mares, having enough experience to know it was safe, were already close, and nuzzled me to hurry up and feed them. White Star finally couldn't resist my affection and came close enough for me to touch him.

God's power courses through the universe, naturally sustaining all that is. It causes no shocks or pain, until it comes in contact with sin. That's why no one has seen the face of the Father, except the Son. That's why Moses' face turned white at seeing only the backside of God as He passed before him on Mt. Sinai. And we, grounded as we are in our sinful nature, cannot approach God directly. We cannot stand the glory of His Being. Yet missing us profoundly, He sent His Son Jesus to cross over into the muddy world of sin.

But now in Christ Jesus ye who sometimes were far off are made nigh by the blood of Christ. For he is our peace, who hath made both one, and hath broken down the middle wall of partition between us (Ephesians 2:13-14).

...Now then we are ambassadors for Christ, as though God did beseech you by us: we pray you in Christ's stead, be ye reconciled to God. For he hath made him to be sin for us, who knew no sin; that we might be made the righteousness of God in him (2 Corinthians 5:20-21).

The Root of Jesse

My friend, Al Stockton, used his huge excavator this summer to transplant some mature apple trees. He prepared the new location with a generous hole. With just one scoop he dug out a tree and placed it in the new hole. He did this twice and then went about the other projects for which he had come.

The transplanted apple trees went into shock, as most living things do when they are transplanted.

You should see Suzanne when we are in the process of moving! She is utterly certain that the rest of her life is going to be miserable, characterized by the permanent loss of all friends and meaningful employment. All the memories of her turbulent childhood and all the insecure feelings of those traumatic childhood moves resurface. When her stepfather's bar bills would accumulate it would be time to move to a different neighborhood and start over. Her needs weren't taken into consideration. The devil, in a bartender's apron, would run her out of her home and school, away from her friends, and chase her to a foreign neighborhood.

Now with the control of our lives given over to God, Suzanne knows that there are good reasons when we move from time to time to new responsibilities in the building of the Kingdom. There has always been plenty of evidence for this in each of our many moves. I remember when we arrived in Fortuna people showed up, some not even church members, to help us unload the moving van and I remember some especially sweet ladies scrubbed our kitchen cupboards clean while their husbands unloaded the truck. Wonderful things have happened in our moves revealing how God has blessed us each step of the way. Remembering this helps us to get over the shock of being transplanted. We love our church family all the more because of these things.

As for our two apple trees, we'll have to wait until spring to see if there was enough vitality stored up in their roots to make them bloom again. They may not make it. But you and I can be grafted onto the Lord of Life Himself, the everlasting Root of Jesse, from which springs up eternal life. Our souls can withstand the heat of any summer, the trauma of any move and the neglect of any childhood losses because of our life-giving, sustaining Messiah. Thank you God for sending us your Son! *And again, Esaias saith, There shall be a root of Jesse, and he that shall rise to reign over the Gentiles; in him shall the Gentiles trust* (Romans 15:12).

Between the Storms

Does God ever seem to be hidden from you, as if there was no caring or help from heaven? Then, at other times, do you feel victorious over all the evils in this world, like God is especially close, as if the sun is shining so brightly on your soul, though the sky all around you might be full of clouds? Do you feel God is close to you, like you are on a road that is perfectly maintained and has had all the bumps cleared away and potholes cleared away?—your friends are calling on the telephone asking you over for dinner, your spouse and children are cheerful and doing their house chores without being asked? Does God seem close to you? Do you sense His power?

Then at other times do you find yourself feeling as if God has just gone away, like the sun behind a cloud right before a picnic or outdoor wedding? The sky darkens. A chill comes over the air. Sin seems more plausible and stuff of the Spirit seems simply religious, like a fad or a sitcom from the 70's, strange and out-of-touch with present reality. You may feel very alone at times like these.

Did you know that the reality is that many people

experience such ups and downs in their walk with God? A lot of it depends upon your temperament and how you interpret your own moods. Did you know many of God's closest prophets felt just like you do at times?

Isaiah felt totally useless in God's plan (Isaiah 53:1); Ezekiel felt bitter and depressed and felt that it was God's fault (Ezekiel 3:14); Habakkuk felt that God had abandoned him at a time when he was so depressed he could only see the bad things in the world around him and that his prayers were unheard (Habakkuk. 1:2).

We are in good company when we struggle in our faith. King David, whom God called "a man after My own heart" wrote: *"How long shall I take counsel in my soul, having sorrow in my heart daily? How long shall mine enemy be exalted over me"* (Psalm 13:2)?

The alternative is to live a life where we pretend nothing really bothers us. We can use our spirituality to anesthetize our feelings, to deaden our senses. Faith is not a way to escape the reality of difficult things but a way to see beyond them to a better eventual outcome controlled by the awesome power of the Creator Himself.

Gratefully we, spiritual Israel, are not judged by our changing feelings and moods, but we are made stronger by coping with them. *And he said, Thy name shall be called no more Jacob, but Israel: for as a prince hast thou struggled with God and with men, and hast prevailed* (Genesis 32:28).

Christian Decision Making

One of the easiest ways for a church to remain peaceful is for its members to do nothing. Then there is nothing to complain about except that nothing is happening. However, people don't complain very often about too little happening. If they speak out too loudly they might be asked why THEY don't do something! Often a church that is doing very little feels rather comfortable, but a church that is doing very little can often begin to decay. Inactivity breeds disease.

Our Fortuna church broke out of the temptation to keep the comfortable status quo many times. We built an amazingly modern and well-equipped school, which has taught thousands of young Christians. We built a wonderful gymnasium complex. We have built a 20,000 square foot community services and homeless center that is unique and beyond the dreams of less bold churches. We have built a sanctuary with both quality and beauty.

About twenty-seven years ago some thought that the quarter-century old building was in need of refurbishing. There were those who thought it was fine just the way it was, but the church was remodeled. Church members have shared with me how, despite the fact that there were strong feelings about this remodel, the church did pull together and maintained a healthy unity.

Twenty-five years have passed and there are those that would like to see the church beautified and some improvements made. Just like twenty-five years ago, there are those that think the church is fine just the way it is. Some things never change!

Another way of keeping the peace other than by not risking doing anything bold, is to respect one another even when we have all have different views. This isn't a natural thing to do because our nature is to fight for what we want and to be apathetic or hostile to what others want. *"But when Sanballat, Tobiah, the Arabs, the Ammonites and the men of Ashdod heard that the repairs to Jerusalem's walls had gone ahead and that the gaps were being closed, they were very angry* (Nehemiah 4:7).

Only Christ can give us the power to respect someone who thinks differently than we do. So what should you do if you want changes made? What should you do if you don't want changes made? Speak out. Clearly and carefully speak out to your elders, board members, and committee members. Tell them what you think should be changed and what you think should be preserved, and why. Listen to what others think and try to understand why they have the opinions they do. When decisions are made at the committee, board, and business session levels, participate. Share your ideas and listen to the ideas of others and participate when votes are taken. When the church makes a decision, support it. Unless it violates spiritual principles, accept what the church decides cheerfully. Thank God we don't all think alike! This way, through the process of Christian decision-making, the Holy Spirit can work His will and then we can go forward and accomplish great things. By keeping our eyes on Christ during the process of decision-making, *"...you and I may be mutually encouraged by each other's faith"* (Romans 1:12).

The Birthday Goat

Dennis May, the same friend I've mentioned before, gave me a goat for my birthday a few months ago. He didn't know it was my birthday, so I suspect it was a sacrificial guilt offering for taking so long to build the goat fence for which I had already traded him my old Dodge diesel pickup. Or maybe he just happened upon an unwanted goat and knew I was anxious to get some of those brush-eating creatures working on the overgrown, steep sides of my property. Since the fence wasn't finished, he took the gift goat home with him when he finished work for the day.

Dennis showed up a couple of months later with some friends. He was so certain they would finish the fence that he brought along a second goat someone had given him. Thinking he would have the fence finished within a day or two, he tied up the goats and left them, instructing me to keep their ropes from getting too tangled.

Within hours the goats were so tangled up they could barely move. Apparently goats aren't intelligent enough to run around a bush in the opposite direction to untangle themselves. I untangled their ropes; they tangled them again. I untied them, hoping the uncompleted fencing would keep them in the general area where they would be safe, but apparently they do have the intelligence to find the smallest little gap between strands in the old section of barbed-wire fencing.

Finally, I developed a new plan. I tied the goat that kept getting out to a fence post right in front of my living room window. Then I could check on him without walking all the way down the side of the hill. This seemed to work fine for a while. Much later in the day, while we were entertaining company, I looked out the window and noticed the goat was completely gone, leash and all. I said, "Oh, no!" to Suzanne and our company. "The goat's gone!"

Jacob, a precocious eleven-year-old, said, "I told you all this morning, the baby horse set him free!"

Jacob had seen this early in the morning and had told the adults in the room, but no one had taken him seriously. With his teeth, White Star had scraped the tied leash upwards on the wooden post until the goat was free. Luckily the goat hid underneath our deck instead of wandering up towards the dangerous highway.

What's the spiritual application here? None that I can think of. Sometimes things just happen. It's tempting to try to find meaning in everything to the point that we're not concentrating on what we should be doing. God wants us to pay attention to what we are doing in this world as well as to be spiritually minded.

If the clouds be full of rain, they empty themselves upon

the earth: and if the tree fall toward the south, or toward the north, in the place where the tree fillet, there it shall be. He that observed the wind shall not sow; and he that regarded the clouds shall not reap (Ecclesiastes 11:3-4).

False Arrest

There really wasn't any good reason for the Missouri State Policemen to have stopped me. It's true that I was a young man with long hair driving a somewhat beat-up looking 1959 MG A sports car. Despite the stereotype I was actually a naive young man who had decided to rejoin the mainstream of American life after leaving the Benedictine Monastery where I had spent the last two years. It was early morning and I was driving home to Chicago from visiting friends south of St. Louis.

The policeman had me in the passenger seat of his patrol car while he was checking out whether my car was stolen. I thought to myself that if he knew what a good person I was he wouldn't be so suspicious, so I tried to make conversation. The nicer I was, the angrier he became until finally he screamed in a threatening voice, "Shut up!" I couldn't believe it. It's not that I hadn't encountered emotional violence before. In the quiet, cloistered hall outside the monastery cafeteria, I had been hit on the head with the edge of a commercial serving spoon by a neurotic priest who sneaked up behind me in the line outside the cafeteria. He thought it was necessary to prevent me from hurting a friend I was goofing around with in line. When he saw the blood running down my forehead, and understood that he had misread the situation, he just walked away angrily to hide his embarrassment.

I just couldn't understand why this policeman next to me in the squad car was so angry; I hadn't done anything wrong. I felt that it should have been obvious that I was a good person. I left the monastery, not to rebel, but to pursue greater freedom and to explore a world of truth that I felt was just outside my reach. And here was this policeman treating me like a criminal. My I. D. checked out and he angrily and abruptly let me go, almost disappointed that I wasn't a criminal.

Have you ever suffered injustice at the hand of authority? Have teachers ever treated you unfairly? Has a boss ever taken his problems out on you? Jesus knows how you're feeling. He knowingly chose a path that would bring the unjust condemnation of the authorities. His life stood for purity and truth, but He received ugly jeers and ridicule. Thank God that Christ was willing to be treated unfairly so that we might have the eternal life He earned by His perfect life.

He never yielded to sin but received the punishment for all sinners. For he hath made him to be sin for us, who knew no sin; that we might be made the righteousness of God in him (2 Corinthians 5:22).

Being Still

I couldn't believe he hit him with his truck. White Star didn't hear Dennis inching up behind him, as he stood blocking the driveway. Dennis had just finished working on the goat fence and was anxious to go home. He had trained his own horses to stay out of his way when he drove down his driveway through the horse pasture surrounding his house. But my horses had no such training because their pasture was fenced off from the driveway. White Star was totally startled by the bump, but not hurt in the least. To Dennis's credit, White Star will probably pay much more attention to cars and trucks in the future, and see them as something to avoid, but it's not the method I would have necessarily used.

At least not on a day when I had my horse-lover friends, Pam and Kristin Badzik, over to help me do some ground work training on the colt. He's only had a halter on him once before. I already had his foster mother, Hey Girl, and his auntie YooHooTwo tied up and occupied with some hay. When I tried to put the halter on White Star he bolted and ran behind the trailer, turned and ran behind Hey Girl, jumped and pushed past Dennis, ran behind the cedar and did everything possible other than let anyone touch him.

I didn't want to give up on the opportunity to have my friends help me with his training so I kept trying to get his attention and calm him down. He knew me. He knew he didn't have anything to fear from me. Usually he would come to me for some loving, pushing between me and another horse in order to get it all for himself. But he would have none of it today. Finally, at Dennis's advice, we gave up.

Dennis went home. Pam and Kristin just stood around and talked horse talk, while grooming and saddling the two mares. White Star calmed down more and more. Finally, I bent toward him and said "Kiss?" He responded by rubbing his velvety nose on my face. We were back on track. After rubbing him and talking to him he calmed down enough to where he accepted the halter and the rope as if he had always worn one. We had a very productive training session.

God has plans to train us into suitable citizens for the Kingdom of God. Sometimes well-intentioned people may bump into us and make us skittish about His plans. Sometimes the hard knocks of life itself may make us nervous and even afraid of letting anyone approach us. God is wise enough to be patient and to gently call us to His side. God tells us to *Be still and know that I am God* (Psalm 46:10). Trusting God overcomes fear and leads us to peace beyond comprehension. *Blessed is the man that trusteth in the LORD, and whose hope the LORD is. For he shall be as a tree planted by the waters, and that spreadeth out her roots by the river, and shall not see when heat cometh, but her leaf shall be green; and shall not be careful in the year of drought, neither shall cease from yielding fruit* (Jeremiah 17:7-8).

Where Have All the Angels Gone?

We are warned not to worship angels, but I can understand how some people might be tempted. Mystical beings hovering unseen just outside our awareness, sent by God to protect us and to wage war on our behalf against the denizens of darkness, are more than welcome in my life.

Angels aren't always invisible, nor do they exist only in the spiritual world, the Bible tells us. We are to entertain strangers with love and caring because, like Abraham, we may be entertaining angels unaware. Isn't that amazing to think about? The man with the sign, "Will work for food," though probably a victim of a poor lifestyle choice, might be an angel testing our hospitality. Even more sobering is the thought that it might be Jesus Himself testing us. *For I was a hungered, and ye gave me meat: I was thirsty, and ye gave me drink: I was a stranger, and ye took me in* (Matthew 25:35).

Most of the people I stop for on the road or take into my house haven't been angels, unless angels like camera equipment. Then maybe this one hitchhiker who left with my Olympus 110, including the telephoto lens, was an angel. But I'd rather never have a camera again than turn away one holy being sent by God.

Angels are primarily messengers of God (Rev. 14:6). God's church has the unique purpose of sharing the last three messages from God before Jesus Christ returns. These are the "Three Angels' Messages" found in Revelation 14. While we know that angels masquerade as men, isn't it amazing that the church functions as a heavenly angel, communicating messages of love on God's behalf before He returns to take His children home? We don't need to worry over the outcome of the seeds we sow, though we want to sow them with love and tend them with care. I wonder how many angels there are to bolster our every effort made on God's behalf? ... *the harvest is the end of the world; and the reapers are the angels* (Matthew 13:39).

Goat Food

Who wants to hear about horses all the time? No one. Especially when there are goats to write about. Goats are newsworthy too, don't you think? My friend, Al, and I finally did our long-talked-about goat deal. Not only did Al sell me a herd of goats but he threw in a deworming shot and hoof-trimming session.

I felt rather draconian waiting outside his livestock trailer with a needle dripping with medicine for each new arrival as it first set its horny feet on its new pasture. I don't think it was necessarily the best way to begin a friendship. But if the shots didn't alarm them, having their hooves trimmed certainly did. Imagine two huge creatures, grabbing you by one of your arms and by one of your legs and, while you are struggling with all your might to get away, they throw you on your side, stick you with a sharp, pointed thing, and start cutting the bottoms of your feet off!

It should come as no surprise to learn that the new goats would not come to me when I went down to their pasture to get acquainted. They probably wondered what new tortures I had devised in the intervening hours since they first arrived. "Heeeeeheeee's baaaaaaack!" the nearest one warned the others. "Looooooook ahhhhhhoooooout! HEEEEEEEeeeeee's caaaaaaaaaming baaaaaaack!" the others joined in as they scattered.

Al told me to feed them grain so that they would come to me in case they got out of their pasture. If I tried to simply catch them, it would be impossible. If they learned to associate me with grain, they'd follow me wherever I went. It worked, of course. Even the three-month-old babies followed their mothers almost close enough for me to pet them.

Jesus called himself the ... *bread of life: he that cometh to me shall never hunger; and he that believeth on me shall never thirst* (John 6:35). God wants us to come to Him where we will be safe from harm forever. By sending His Son to us as the Bread of Life God reveals to us His complete intentions. The sweetness of Christ's Spirit then draws us in, fills us with wonder and hope, and feeds our hungry souls.

Pregnant or Possibly Plump

My two mares were bred last year and I dutifully recorded their due dates in my calendar. When horses become pregnant, they don't tell you whether they have morning sickness, and they don't request special treats like pickles and peanut butter. Home pregnancy tests don't work well because the horses just don't cooperate! To pay a vet for the privilege of knowing if my horses are pregnant isn't within my budget.

My mares looked full in the belly, and, since one of them was still nursing her foster colt, I made sure to feed them all enough grain. I was looking forward to having some more babies around. Like all babies, they are so rewarding to be around. Since horse babies are extra big, it's an extra big blessing.

The due date came and went — no baby. With all the rain there was lots of grass to eat in the pasture. I slowed down and then stopped the grain feeding. Their tummies got slimmer and slimmer — still no babies. So, unless I couldn't count to eleven months, or the foals were incredibly late, my horses were just a little plump and not very pregnant.

Our lives can seem pregnant with promise, too, but just be a little spiritually overfed. How do we know our lives are going to produce fruit? We cannot know because of how much spiritual food we eat. We cannot know because of how much fruit we may seem to be producing, because only God knows the outcome of the harvest. The fields we sow today may become full of weeds tomorrow. We can only know that our lives will produce fruit if our hope is based, not on what we eat or see, but on the promises of God. *For the promise is unto you, and to your children, and to all that are afar off, even as many as the LORD our God shall call* (Acts 2:39). Our role is limited to responding to God's initiative in reaching out to us, and saying "yes!" We don't need to worry about the fruit; we just need to focus on saying, "yes!" to His promises.

Hospital Humor

Why write so much about horses and goats? Two reasons: one, they never retaliate with embarrassing stories about me; two, they never think that I am mean when I point out their follies. People are different. We have a silly notion that we should look good in front of others. We all know that we are nothing to speak of when we are at home in our torn underwear, but we want others to think well of us in public.

There's one notable exception: when we are in the hospital after a surgery and we are full of pain medication. We loosen up a bit then and even give permission for our antics to be broadcast without any regard to copyright or pride.

Take my friend Lorraine Schueler, for example. She knows how to keep confidences and I assume that she expects her confidences to be kept in return. I say "assume" because she's never actually asked me to keep anything confidential, but she did specifically say that she would tell others about the disposable cup incident. She can't very well expect me to keep that quiet if she is planning to tell it to whomever she pleases.

It was the second day she was in rehab after her hip surgery. She was sitting up and reading a newspaper when Suzanne and I arrived to see her again.

Lorraine isn't your average recuperator. She had already been laughing, making jokes, and refusing to worry about how long her recovery might take, even though it was clear her recovery would take longer than she had hoped. She had this mechanical extension-grabbing device, with a handle to squeeze so the ends could be manipulated to grab objects. Take Lorraine's personality, add a touch of pain medication and a device like that, and you have trouble. Lorraine thought it was particularly funny to reach out toward a person affectionately giving the shoulder a little squeeze. She did this first to Suzanne, then to me. The nurses didn't seem to come into her room a lot.

When we remarked on the device, Lorraine was eager to show us how adept she was at it already. She grabbed a Styrofoam cup filled with water and began to raise it to her lips. Squeezing the trigger a tad too tightly, she punched the mechanical thumb right through the large cup, soaking the table and floor. She thought it was hilarious – so funny, in fact that she reported to me later that she had repeated the adventure later that evening with a milk shake. *A merry heart doeth good like a medicine: but a broken spirit drieth the bones* (Proverbs 17:22). This applies not only to healing postoperatively; it's an earmark of a person healing from all sorts of things, physically, mentally, and spiritually. It's okay to laugh at the silliness of the fallen human condition first in ourselves and in others. The release may free us to take God and His goodness more seriously.

Not Too Busy To Care

I love the challenge of working on a large team to provide the thousands of people who gather annually for Redwood Camp Meeting in Northern California with an uplifting spiritual experience. It is a challenge, which an amazing amount of self-sacrificing volunteers take up. There's also full time volunteers who, like the Camp Director, Don Charlton, work hard throughout the year to make sure the camp is ready to receive the flood of people who come seeking a blessing from the speakers and the fellowship.

It has always been a busy time for me. For thirteen years I coordinated the Junior Division, keeping as many as two hundred 10-12 year-olds safe and involved in spiritually nurturing events. The positive atmosphere of teamwork with other motivated pastors was always exhilarating to me. For the last three years I have chaired the main pavilion, organizing the presenters and participants for up to six meetings per day. It is good work and very busy at times. It's also fun to interact with so many positive, exciting people.

Coming home one night—one advantage of living not too far away from the camp meeting—I noticed that one of my horses had torn one of his legs on the barbed wire fence, or in some other foolish way that yearling stallions find to fill up their days. Since White Star was an orphan and required a lot of care as a young colt, I am very bonded to him. His wound looked bad, about the size of a dollar bill torn in half. I was so busy with camp meeting duties that I needed help from my rancher friend, Dennis. He brought his large livestock trailer over so that I wouldn't have to struggle with teaching a yearling to board a little horse trailer.

During the day or two while all this was happening and until I heard from the vet that my horse would be fine, I was upset. The memory of how it felt when my horse found some comfort after his surgery by keeping his frightened muzzle against my arm stayed with me. With all the commotion and responsibilities and with thousands of campers all around me, a portion of my mind was dedicated and reserved for concern of my little horse. After all, his well-being was *my* responsibility.

Isn't that how God feels about each one of us? Isn't that how God feels about you? With the entire universe to rule, His mind and heart are large enough to have a space just for me and just for you. Our hurts occupy His mind; He is not going about business as usual and will not return to business as usual until we are healed, until all his children who are willing, come out of their pain and out of danger and darkness.

Thy mercy, O LORD, is in the heavens; and Thy faithful-

ness reacheth unto the clouds. Thy righteousness is like the great mountains; Thy judgments are a great deep: O LORD, Thou preservest man and beast. How excellent is Thy loving kindness, O God! Therefore the children of men put their trust under the shadow of Thy wings (Psalm 36:5-7).

Reopening Wounds

The skin was torn pretty badly on White Star's back leg, leaving an open wound about the size of a dollar bill torn in half. I had already taken him to the vet and afterwards to my rancher friend, Dennis, who took White Star home with him to "doctor him up." I was hesitant to kneel down next to my unbroken, 1200 pound stallion to do the painful things that needed to be done.

Horses heal differently than people. Their scar tissue gets very thick and a granulation occurs in the tissue that can make for very deforming lumps. If the wound on the front of the back leg had been left to heal on its own, it would have formed such a big lump that the front hoof would have hit it whenever the horse was galloping.

You have to wonder if the cure was worse than the malady. The newly-forming granulating wound has to be scrubbed open. A chemical found in Adolph's meat tenderizer—my friend actually uses Adolph's—is sprinkled on the abnormally thickened, fleshy area where the enzymes and the scrubbing reduce the wound closer to its original condition. The wound is then oiled with an antibiotic lotion and bandaged. Each time this is done, the normal skin has an opportunity to grow a little closer on each side of the wound. The wound is almost half-way closed now, with healthy hair-covered skin where an ugly, hardened scar would have been.

What wounds do you have that may have been scarred over, making some of the edges where you come into contact with others hard and unfeeling? God, too, will reopen the wounds if you hold still and trust Him. He will remove the coarse scars of a cold heart and make new flesh grow, flesh that is warm to the touch and that can feel.

My wounds stink and are corrupt because of my foolishness (Psalm 38:5). *From the sole of the foot even unto the head there is no soundness in it; but wounds, and bruises, and putrefying sores: they have not been closed, neither bound up, neither mollified with ointment* (Isaiah 1:6). *He healeth the broken in heart, and bindeth up their wounds* (Psalm 147:3).

Wonderfully Made

Al Stockton's goats had their babies at his place only fives miles away from my ranch. Though he's closer to the ocean, the climate couldn't be that much different. I was beginning to doubt that my does were pregnant after all. Maybe their udders hadn't swollen as much as I had thought, and I just wasn't going to get any babies. My mares had tricked me into feeding them extra grain all winter and spring only to get fat with no foals at all. Maybe my goats had learned from them.

A few days ago, in the middle of all that rain, one of my goats didn't come for her feed. When I looked for her, she had two babies with her. They were tiny little white goats shivering in the rain, asleep on the muddy hillside.

If I had a barn, I would not have trusted nature at all. I would have put them inside away from the rain. Then I noticed that the mother kept walking away, leaving one or both of them all alone while she browsed the hillside, sometimes two or three hundred yards away. Clutching one, I put it under my coat and carried it closer to the mother who didn't seem very disturbed by the return of her missing baby. A neighbor noticing the whole thing, observed the goat didn't seem to have any mothering instincts at all.

The reality was that the mother goat knew something we didn't. God made these funny creatures wonderfully suited to their station and place in life. Their hair, fully grown in at birth, is comprised of hollow core fibers which insulate very well even while wet. The mother leaves them while they sleep because she needs to eat constantly in order to produce a prodigious amount of rich milk. Her babies are also born much more developed than some babies are. They are able to walk and even to play with their brother or sister almost immediately! Even the shivering produces heat to keep them warm.

Although death is a sad and terrible part of nature in this sinful world, God has made all living creatures with an astounding capacity to survive and thrive. This tendency to thrive is built into us as well, and it would be good to remember that when we worry about our health. Although modern medicine is nothing short of miraculous sometimes our role is just to acknowledge how wonderfully we are made and to cooperate with God's design and His natural laws of health and wellness.

For thou hast possessed my reins: thou hast covered me in my mother's womb. I will praise thee; for I am fearfully and wonderfully made: marvelous are thy works; and that my soul knoweth right well (Psalm 139:13-14).

Our Real Big Brother

My neighbor's dog loves to harass my goats. The mature ones know he is bluffing, but the babies get really scared. The dog cornered them by the tool shed, near where the babies squeeze through the fence. They can get through where the adult goats can't. The baby goats were running away from the dog using the same technique they use with me. They run around the shed just one corner ahead of me each go around. Usually I get tired after a few circuits, or maybe I just lose any illusions about the chances of success and give up. But the dog wasn't getting winded or disillusioned and kept going until the babies would dive into the slit in the field fencing. The problem was that in order for the goats to get through, they had to hunch up their shoulders, wiggle through part way, then suck in their breath or do something that requires some presence of mind to get the rest of the way through. In their panic, they kept on diving into the gap, almost bouncing back.

My friend Laurie was watching the whole thing from the bathroom window and relating to me each turn of events. I was getting ready to preach an unfinished multimedia sermon. I knew the dog pretty well and knew that he has never bitten any of the animals at the neighboring ranches, so I didn't feel like I could really afford the time to do anything about it.

The baby goats, however, did not know any of this and were crying out for protection. To Laurie's amazement, Hey Girl, the matriarch mare of the hillside, came over and stood right up to the fence. The dog stopped barking and backed off. Hey Girl started to wander away and the dog immediately resumed harassing the baby goats. Hey Girl turned around and stood again right up to the edge of the field fence near the ruckus until the dog gave up and went home.

I wish I had Hey Girl to protect me back when I was a kid growing up in Chicago. When I was 12 years old, I moved from the suburbs to the inner city of Chicago. I had a pack of bullies pick up on my lack of city swagger and harass me to no end.

Showing up in school one day with a penny in the slit of each of my new penny loafers, didn't help things at all. Ralph, the perennially retained 7th grader who was as hairy as a tarantula and had eyes like a Colombian drug lord—both friendly and dangerous like someone who enjoys hurting people—discovered my faux pas. Immediately, the lunch line turned vicious, like sharks smelling blood in the water. My memory fails me, mercifully, at this point in the story. I do remember something about losing my new winter coat, and being taunted with a knife just to amuse and impress the crowd.

When I told my family what had happened, my older brother was dispatched to stop by my school the next day. He would be passing by there anyway on his way to doing drugs or burglarizing some place, or however he spent his days after dropping out of high school. This was before a judge gave him the choice of going to jail or enlisting in the army. He gave the whole wild pack a good tough talking to. It was then that my life took a very dangerous downturn. I became known as the one who tried to intimidate them with my big brother. I'll let your imagination fill in the rest of the story of what last school year was like!

No one can really protect you from bullies in this dog-eat-dog world. But, there is someone out of this world who can—Jesus. Just the mention of his name makes bullies tremble, dogs swallow their barks, and the picked-on take heart. The power of His presence makes the demons inhabit pigs and jump over cliffs, makes the meek in spirit inherit the earth, and can make you conquer all your fears. *For I am persuaded, that neither death, nor life, nor angels, nor principalities, nor powers, nor things present, nor things to come, Nor height, nor depth, nor any other creature, shall be able to separate us from the love of God, which is in Christ Jesus our Lord* (Romans 8:38-39).

Pray Without Ceasing

If we think we understand God's will for us but are unhappy, competitive or unproductive in our family or church life, we are missing something.

As a minister, I've listened to people who are so sure that their particular interpretation of scripture, or their view of how the building project should go, are correct that they are willing to go to unproductive extremes, even crusades within their church, to make sure everyone agrees with them. Luckily, not in my present church, but elsewhere I have seen those rare hurting ones accost visitors, abuse speakers, and isolate themselves from people whom God could otherwise use to encourage and uplift them. But no, they claim, they do not need any encouragement. God has assured them that they are correct. They will do anything but listen. They don't understand how key listening is.

Many Christians believe in the reformation maxim, *sola scriptura*, which means that it is by the scriptures alone we may understand the truth about God. Others believe that the Holy Spirit guides them so intimately that they are either "impressed" with the truth of a scripture or not. It seems this might lead some to believe things that are really out of harmony with the scriptures. What is your position?

I believe that scripture is the yardstick, the cognitive reality against which we must measure our thoughts about all things. I believe that the Holy Spirit moves us to consider this measuring in the first place and is the very cause of our interest in spiritual things to begin with.

In these stories about country life you may have noticed that behind the events, the author is listening for spiritual meanings. This is one way I honor the scripture that says, "Pray unceasingly." If praying unceasingly means something we do with our lips, there would be little to separate us from some of the unfortunate street people suffering from schizophrenia who carry on animated conversations with unseen people.

God doesn't want us to go around mumbling constantly to Him or anyone else. He wants us engaged productively in this world. Remember, the Fourth Commandment isn't just about rest. "...Six days shalt thou labour and do all thy work."

Although God wants us actively engaged in productive work, He does also want us to pray unceasingly. To me this means constantly listening to Him. If you are like me, you are tempted to think of prayer only as something that we *do*. Prayer is telling God things. If that is all prayer is, then it seems a little pointless because God already knows everything we could possibly tell Him. Of course, there is a blessing in our turning to God with all of our concerns and cares and praise but since He knows our heart already there must be more to praying unceasingly than just telling Him what He already knows.

Some people would say that to pray unceasingly means to think about and to repeat scriptures in our minds while we do our daily tasks. Although the repetition of scriptures can be encouraging and uplifting and can shape our thoughts to be healthy and Godly, we cannot do that *constantly* or we would have a half conscious, out-of-focus mentality. I think God wants to speak to us in the daily drama of life itself, and our listening to Him constitutes a part of our "praying unceasingly."

The Holy Spirit moves us to hear God's still small voice through the circumstances of our lives; the scriptures offer us a way of measuring and comparing our insights with objective truth, both correcting and directing our minds toward a refined spiritual perception.

This is a simple way of looking at things but not a simplistic way. It's an integrated approach to a spiritual and physical life, an un-compartmentalized approach to spirituality. If God has spoken to you through these stories, He can speak to you through the common events in your life, too. Listen to Him. Compare what you're hearing with the scriptures to define your sense of truth. Become spiritually engaged in all you do. It's the good life! *Rejoice evermore. Pray without ceasing. In every thing give thanks: for this is the will of God in Christ Jesus concerning you* (1 Thessalonians 5:16-18).